THE MIRACLE
OF
DIVINE LOVE HEALING

by

Robert G. Fritchie

World Service Institute, Knoxville, Tennessee
Copyright © 2022 Robert G. Fritchie

Published in the United States by World Service Institute.

Disclaimer: The author of this book does not dispense medical advice or prescribe the use of any technique as a form of treatment for physical, emotional, spiritual or medical problems without the advice of a physician, either directly or indirectly. The intent of the author is only to offer information of a nature to help you in your quest for spiritual, emotional and physical well-being. In the event you use the information in this book for yourself, which is your constitutional right, the author, publisher, printer and distributors assume no responsibility for your actions.

Cover photo: Point Lobos State Natural Reserve, California

ISBN 9780997690538
Fritchie, Robert G.
The Miracle of Divine Love Healing
1st edition 2022
1. Mind and body.   2. Spirituality.   3. Spiritual Healing.
4. Self-Healing Techniques.   5. Self-Help Techniques.

TABLE OF CONTENTS

"There is a light in this world,
a healing spirit more powerful
than any darkness we may encounter.
We sometimes lose sight of this force
when there is suffering,
too much pain."

- Mother Teresa

PREFACE

"Miracle" - A surprising and welcome event that is not explicable by natural or scientific laws and is therefore considered to be the work of a divine agency."

(Oxford Languages Dictionary)

"Divine" - "Connected with a god."

(Cambridge Dictionary)

"Love" - "An intense feeling of deep affection."

(Oxford Languages Dictionary)

"Healing" - "The process of becoming well again, especially after a cut or other injury, or of making someone well again."

(Cambridge Dictionary)

We begin this book with four definitions that help explain the meaning of the book title THE MIRACLE OF DIVINE LOVE HEALING. We do this to make sure you understand that we are talking about a spiritual process that involves the Creator of the universe (God) and Divine Love, which is the Creator's energy made available to enable healing of persons, places, or things.

We have taught the miracle of Divine Love since 1981 and have achieved excellent results as our 2018 AT ONENESS HEALING SYSTEM ADVANCED PROTOCOL evolved.

Right now, many countries of the world are experiencing an increase in illness. These illnesses appear so suddenly, with health declining so rapidly, that people do not have time to assess what has happened to them before becoming incapacitated. Our intention in this book is to give you Divine Love spiritual healing methods you can apply now, to avoid becoming sick, and to heal side effects and other illnesses.

The solutions being provided are more powerful than any of our past teachings about the application of Divine Love because you will be rapidly aligned with the Creator and Divine will, facilitating a faster healing response.

This book is organized into eight chapters that show how to obtain improved healing results.

Chapter One, **The Current Reality,** explains the health dilemmas we are all facing.

Chapter Two, **Healing DNA and Energetic Blocks with Divine Love,** explains what is happening to us and what we can do to correct the problems.

Chapter Three, **The Miracle of Divine Love Healing Reality Principles,** explains how spirit interacts with the energy of the Creator (called Divine Love) to effect change. These inter-actions represent 13 key energy principles to help you understand how to be more effective in your own self-healing.

Chapter Four, **Attain the Miracle of Divine Love Healing in Your Life,** explains six critical topics/principles to achieve lasting healing.

Chapter Five, **Healing Neurological Issues,** reveals for the first time how to heal the brain.

Chapter Six, **Behind the Scenes of Divine Love Healing,** presents critical information to deepen your knowledge base.

Chapter Seven, **The Largest Miracle,** provides a solution for recovering from the side effects of COVID and other illnesses.

Chapter Eight, **Problem Solving with the Miracle of Divine Love,** presents a method people can apply to minimize discord, both personally and throughout the world.

For students interested in the scientific and spiritual approaches to ancient technologies, an Addendum contains some additional healing techniques we have modified to work more effectively. The Addendum includes:

Removing Dimensional Vibrations explains how to remove hidden detrimental energy effects. This topic is important for physicians to understand when patients do not respond well to medical treatment.

Chakra and Thymus Healing Methods discusses two alternative techniques healing with Divine Love. These tools are useful if you choose to use other energy healing methods to recover your health.

Please read this book in the order presented for a better foundation of understanding, and to build personal self confidence in using the techniques of Divine Love spiritual healing.

"Spirituality is recognizing and celebrating that we are all inextricably connected to each other by a power greater than all of us, and that our connection to that power and to one another is grounded in love and compassion. Practicing spirituality brings a sense of perspective, meaning and purpose to our lives."

- Brené Brown

CHAPTER 1

THE CURRENT REALITY

With the release of the self help book DYNAMIC REALITIES AND DIVINE LOVE HEALING and our key teaching video, THE ADVANCED PROTOCOL AND HEALING STATEMENT TRAINING VIDEO, our primary goal of bringing healing with Divine Love information to the public was achieved. We thought that further books would be unnecessary, but we were mistaken.

The emergence of the COVID virus has been accompanied by widespread fear. In turn, that fear has introduced additional psychological trauma into people's lives.

As a result, too many people feel they have lost their sense of freedom, further increasing their fears, and are now suffering physically, mentally, and spiritually. While an abundance of information and solutions have been promoted around the world, not all have been helpful.

It is not my intent to engage in a discussion about treatment effectiveness or the rightness or wrongness of various medical treatments. Likewise, religious preferences and beliefs, age, gender, nationality, financial situation, health, science, or other social topics that may influence solutions to health problems will not be discussed.

However, we should not ignore the world reports that indicate human DNA may have become changed after COVID vaccinations, as evidenced by the appearance of side effects. Many scientists believe these side effects are neither reversible nor treatable.

I asked the Creator what could be done to help people who displayed side effects and was told:

➢ *If a person asks the Creator for help, the Creator will restore that person to the health condition they had before COVID appeared. Parents can ask for help as proxies for minor children under the age of 16.*

➢ *Further improvement in each person's health condition is initiated by asking the Creator for specific help.*

➢ *Decisions to restore or not restore health are the Creator's.*

Why this strong response from the Creator?

Medical researchers consider the sudden appearance of life-threatening illnesses being reported worldwide to be a precursor to major health problems. Or, perhaps we are dealing with the appearance of biochemical effects in our cellular structure which may not be reversible, and which may affect human health for many years.

Is there a real solution, or are we facing a long-term, worldwide deterioration of health? Before that question can be answered, we need to recognize that the Creator of the universe exists, and can help people recover from illness.

The reality of the Creator is vital to our survival; we may have reached the point where mankind cannot recover health without divine intervention from the Creator.

I believe that Divine Love is the only alternative. How do I justify such a bold statement? Well, beginning in 1980, I was led along a spiritual healing research path that over the next 38 years resulted in a spiritual healing system called the AT ONENESS HEALING SYSTEM ADVANCED PROTOCOL. It is a means by which people can apply Divine Love spiritual self-healing techniques.

Teachings are available in a video titled THE ADVANCED PROTOCOL AND HEALING STATEMENT TRAINING VIDEO. The same principles are taught in the book DYNAMIC REALITIES AND DIVINE LOVE HEALING.

People throughout the world, whatever their beliefs or religious background, have successfully utilized the AT ONENESS HEALING SYSTEM ADVANCED PROTOCOL. Prior to the COVID pandemic, we saw amazing results when people correctly applied these healing principles. Since the pandemic began, the healings have continued, but have increased in urgency and complexity.

We have observed that if people believe in a higher power (the Creator of the universe), they usually get good results when applying the Advanced Protocol, but people who do not believe in the Creator seldom get good results.

Once people have used the Advanced Protocol and witnessed positive results, they begin to understand that Divine Love energy is based solely upon spiritual love. If we experience any hate or fear as we use the Advanced Protocol, results are limited until those negative emotions have been released by the Advanced Protocol.

Are you making necessary changes to your unhealthy practices?

You may use our Divine Love methods successfully, but you must continue to be responsible for your own continued wellness, correcting unhealthy practices and releasing any detrimental beliefs.

We can identify our unhealthy practices by consulting books on nutrition and health before or after a healing with Divine Love, but how do you recognize and change damaging beliefs? With all the information we are exposed to today, how do you decide what to believe? And how do you know that what you believe is true?

Are you aware of your untrue beliefs?

Many people rely upon the internet and the media for information and believe much of what they are told, yet even authority figures may not always represent the truth. Perhaps we should challenge those authorities to determine real truth.

Since our spirit is uniquely linked to the Creator of the universe, each of us is capable of discerning truth from within ourselves! Therefore, it would be wise to learn how to ask the Creator if what we are observing and being told is the spiritual and physical truth.

This is important because information from the Creator will always be spiritually and physically true. Once you digest the contents of this book, you will be able to ask for and receive information from within your spiritual essence. This information will come from your intuition via the Creator. We will show how to determine truth later in this book.

We may often wonder how something we fervently believe in our personal lives seems to change over time. Sometimes that changing belief or truth helps us; at other times it seems to restrict our lives. Let's review a few recent developments that impact our truth right now.

Examples of Changing Truths

Untruth: I am limited in what I can do.

This represents one of the largest failures in education today. We should only be limited by what we *believe*. If we are open to change and discovery, we human beings can achieve almost anything, with or without, a formal education. This principle should be taught to every school child.

There are scientific proofs that show that people react to, and become, what they believe. Thus, when the message is positive and uplifting, the individual is encouraged to excel.

If the message is negative and disparaging, the individual may become depressed, which leads to failure, dissatisfaction and underachievement.

Untruth: We cannot exceed the speed of light.
It takes light years to reach a distant star system, yet the science of space will soon be changed because scientists are studying how spacecraft can operate at speeds greater than the speed of light.

Limited truth: Quantum mechanics attempts to explain scientific discrepancies in our physical world that deviate from what is expected in classical physics and chemistry experiments.

Quantum mechanics accounts for conversion of spiritual energy into physical energy. Quantum mechanics will become a tool to help the public better understand how elements and compounds can be changed by altering the frequency at which they oscillate.

In effect, that is what we are doing right now in healing with Divine Love: Altering the frequency specific to a given illness and re-coding cells to achieve wellness. When these two things are done, the body can more rapidly heal itself.

Do we have a spiritual future?

Spirituality can become a source of education. People can learn to work directly with the Creator and the Creator's Angels. We can count on the Creator to guide us as we move forward in this changing world. Angels are spiritual beings serving as divine messengers and intermediaries who can help anyone because they are nondenominational.

Also, as we learn to work properly with Divine Love, we realize that we benefit as we operate in a loving manner to eliminate bias, hatred, and prejudice.

We see the future as a spiritual collection of events that are brought into our physical reality. People are able to improve health and other issues through our AT ONENESS HEALING SYSTEM ADVANCED PROTOCOL. If you have not used or studied the Protocol, take the time to read the books and videos referenced on our main web page: https://www.worldserviceinstitute.org

The references will help you understand how human beings have the capacity to make major changes in their lives when they work in conjunction with the *energy* and support of the Creator. The energy referenced is the Creator's spiritual love (Divine Love).

Divine Love circulates throughout the universe constantly as a neutral energy until activated by a Petition to accomplish something in one's life that needs to be corrected. Healing takes place according to the Creator's will.

When a healing request is not approved by the Creator, or if a person has not asked the Creator for help, the petitions associated with the Advanced Protocol do not engage, and there is no healing.

The Advanced Protocol has been used to successfully heal symptoms only possible with the Creator's involvement. Results are often called *miracles* until people understand the underlying principles. Then Divine Love can become an accepted practice.

I've known people with cancer or other terminal illnesses who used the Advanced Protocol, and in fewer than 10 days they would see a complete remission of the illness, confirmed by medical test.

In other cases, it is evident that the Creator withholds healing. *This may* occur *when the Creator wants a person to recognize the poor life practices that produced the illness.*

Once an individual "gets it," a healing using the Advanced Protocol will usually go rapidly to completion. "Getting it" means that the individual recognizes and decides to replace a poor life practice with a good life practice.

You need to understand additional criteria to preserve your health. We state this not to frighten you, but as a truth to help you avoid severe sudden illnesses and/or death.

The Advanced Protocol has been successfully used for a wide variety of diseases, infections, and viruses, as well as chemical and environmental poisoning and reactions from radiation exposure.

Several years of healing reports written by people using Divine Love methods to recover their health are available on our website at: https://www.worldserviceinstitute.org

Does the medical field resist healing with Divine Love?

If our Divine Love methods are as good as our students report, one might ask why the medical community has not yet embraced these methods and integrated them into modern medicine. From personal observation, I believe that much of the resistance occurs because:

➢ *Divine Love Spiritual Healing is free and is not subject to manipulation.*

➢ *Without research costs or equipment, and very few expenses associated with Divine Love spiritual healing, the opportunity for financial gain is minimal.*

When physicians who believe in the Creator begin to apply the teachings found in this book in their medical practice together with their medical training and experience, all will benefit.

Let's Change Our Reality

The use of medications with short or long-term, side effects no longer needs to be the only option for treatments. Instead, people can learn how to neutralize side effects while using our Divine Love methods. If someone's intention is to correctly use medicines to recover health, then correction of side effects will be allowed.

However, if someone's intention is to continue the *indiscriminate use* of medicines without thorough investigation and scientific study, then side effect healing will not be effective. We must be responsible.

Many people believe that they can take a pill for whatever ails them, without considering the underlying causes of their problems. Such behavior is limiting because we are not taking responsibility for ourselves. And, unfortunately, much of modern medicine focuses upon treating *symptoms*, rather than the *underlying causes* of those symptoms.

The Advanced Protocol addresses both CAUSE AND EFFECT which, in combination with good physicians, usually lead to better health outcomes. These partnerships can be a big win for both patients and providers.

Many technologies are dependent upon accurate application of healing energies. These various technologies are typified by light, electricity, frequency, and biochemical devices. While these all may work, many are still in an evaluation phase. Some even introduce inherent dangers by changing the body's mechanisms, resulting in unexpected deterioration.

The good news is that Divine Love is not subject to such limitations. When we utilize Divine Love in spiritual healing, the right combination of Divine Love energies are automatically provided, thereby preventing the introduction of harmful side effects.

My intent in Divine Love spiritual healing has always been to identify and remove underlying causes of illness and to heal symptoms.

➢   *Divine Love is able to correct all known problems, provided the Creator is willing to heal a symptom we specify.*

Do you understand the differences between the spiritual and the physical kingdoms?

When first introduced to spiritual healing, I knew nothing about Divine Love spiritual energy. For several years my teachers were my Angels. But their teachings were not given in a way that I could easily comprehend. It often seemed as if everything had dual meanings.

I had to learn to differentiate between the *spiritual kingdom,* which has no restrictions, and our physical *kingdom,* which does have some restrictions. The only way I could measure progress was to observe a change in a client and measure that change with currently accepted tests. Sometimes a symptom would be corrected immediately. Some results would be obvious, such as the elimination of pain or the freeing up of a frozen joint. And yet, often the reason people did not get well was unknown.

Eventually we learned the simple explanation:

➢   *People need to verbally express their* **willingness to accept Divine Love within their** **bodies***. Then, the spiritual kingdom and the physical kingdom that we live in merge, and full healing manifests!*

This is a major teaching: You MUST ACCEPT Divine Love for it to work. How to accomplish this is explained in Chapter 4.

In this book you will find an integration of teachings. While some information is taken from previous writings, other material covers topics you may not yet have been exposed to.

Altogether, the information is designed to give you a complete understanding of the healing process and to eliminate any doubts or misunderstandings you might have as to the efficacy of healing with Divine Love.

We Have Made Some Petition Improvements

Previously, petitions were presented in a manner that allowed people to do self-healing slowly.

➤ *We have now modified petitions we refer to in this book to reflect the direct involvement of the Creator, who provides what each person needs.*

This has been done to speed up healing while completely eliminating fear. When you use these modified petitions, you will have very powerful results because it is the Creator directly providing your healing. The Advanced Protocol remains unchanged because it already reflects the direct involvement of the Creator.

"The first peace, which is the most
important, is that which comes
within the souls of people when
they realize their relationship,
their oneness with the universe
and all its powers, and when they
realize at the center of the universe
dwells the Great Spirit and that
its center is really everywhere,
it is within each of us."

- Black Elk

CHAPTER 2

HEALING DNA AND ENERGETIC BLOCKS WITH DIVINE LOVE

We are currently witnessing a major deterioration in the health of the population in general. People have developed many fears about the COVID virus, greatly increasing personal stress, which can then easily overwhelm immune systems.

As a result, previously unidentified health issues have begun to appear. One theory offered by scientists is that the virus has compromised the more susceptible immune systems of people with multiple underlying illnesses, or those who have weakened their immune systems with dangerous lifestyles or exposure to toxic environments.

Below is another perspective that explains why those with compromised immune systems may not readily respond to medical treatment.

Our Altered DNA

In BEING AT ONE WITH THE DIVINE, published in 2014, we discussed *Dimensional Vibrations,* which are one of the underlying causes of abnormal DNA. It is important to know how these and other harmful vibrations (frequencies) affect our current health because much of the altered DNA is correctable using the Advanced Protocol (depending upon the Creator's will).

Our DNA has become modified over time as a result of the environments and experiences of our ancestors. Dimensional Vibrations are the effects of ancient energy.

Unfortunately, many Dimensional Vibrations can create health problems that cannot be treated with conventional medicine. These vibrations may also be very difficult to recognize. A person might experience pain or another symptom for no apparent reason. Sometimes, the underlying cause of a symptom is an ancestral DNA effect now manifesting in the physical body.

Although some DNA abnormalities have been with us since birth, we are concerned with the more recent emergence of adult Dimensional Vibrations, first observed by us in 2010 when extremely sick clients appeared who had not been helped by conventional medicine. Dimensional Vibrations contained in their DNA manifested at odd times, and prevented them from healing.

You may wonder why the word "Dimensional" is used. Here is what I have learned:

➢ *As someone with a significant illness begins to heal using conventional medicine or earlier healing with Divine Love techniques, the energy level of their body rises to a higher vibration (frequency). At that higher vibration, a previously hidden Dimensional Vibration would then fully manifest and prevent further healing.*

When we accept that the Creator and the Angels exist at higher vibrations than ours, we can relate to Dimensional Vibrations being present in the spiritual realm at higher vibrations.

Clients who were not aware of this spiritual condition at the normal vibration levels of their physical bodies often believed their illnesses to be incurable. Once we showed how to identify and release Dimensional Vibrations their illnesses improved.

➢ *Until the Advanced Protocol was released for use in 2018, Dimensional Vibrations were energetically removed using the Divine Love technique described in the Addendum (included for those of you who are interested in the original method.)*

➢ *Today we use the Advanced Protocol exclusively to heal altered DNA, energy blocks,* and any resulting damage to the body from these.

➤   In the Advanced Protocol, Dimensional Vibrations are included as "pop ups." Any pop ups are automatically removed while using the Advanced Protocol.

Many people have chosen to depend on the opinions of conflicted men rather than seeking guidance from the Creator. In addition, when we make unloving choices, we are creating current Dimensional Vibrations! However, healing with Divine Love provides a solution.

Let's Not Forget About Your Energy Blocks!

Two additional phenomena impede healing:

➤   The appearance of increasingly complex emotional energy blocks. Many of these blocks are caused by stress, which raises the cortisol level in the body. Excess cortisol is known to inhibit the immune system, which makes us more vulnerable to illness.

➢   *The toxins in food, air, water, skin products and medicines cause damage to our cells and our DNA.*

It is apparent that in today's environment:

➢   *For permanent healing to take place, all Dimensional Vibrations, energy blocks and toxin damage need to be completely removed.*

In the following chapters, we will show how these conditions can be healed by the Creator with Divine Love.

**"It does not matter how long
you are spending on the earth,
how much money you have gathered or
how much attention you have received.
It is the amount of positive vibration
you have radiated in life that matters."**

- Amit Ray

CHAPTER 3

THE MIRACLE OF DIVINE LOVE HEALING REALITY PRINCIPLES

This chapter gives the reader practical insight into 13 key energy reality principles upon which THE MIRACLE OF DIVINE LOVE HEALING is based. These are presented from the perspective of an engineer who became a spiritual healing scientist.

A 43-year high tech career in the design, development and implementation of advanced digital systems for government and industry disciplined me to investigate, challenge, and explain the healing phenomena to which I had been introduced.

I share here some personal experiences from my first 29 years of energy healing and spiritual healing. This will help you understand that the energy reality principles are based upon proven repeatable experiences.

Reality Principle #1: Current reality is what we can make happen in the present; that reality changes with your experience.

My spiritual journey started with the Japanese martial art of Aikido. We learned how to use "Ki" (spiritual energy) in our bodies to move an opponent using only minimal contact; to enter a fully conscious state where we could endure heat, cold and pain resulting from direct punches and nerve holds. We also learned to apply "Ki" to promote rapid recovery from injuries such as joint dislocations.

While it was obvious Aikido tapped an unseen energy that could be called upon to produce physical effects, the *how* and *what* of that energy was not explained. Students of Ki, Qi (Chi), Prana, shaman energy, North American Indian Medicine as well as Reiki masters access the same universal energy source at various levels, depending upon their training and personal energy. The concept of Divine Love energy was not evident in most of those energy approaches prior to 1980.

Reality Principle #2: We can transmit energy through space with directed intention.

In the fall of 1979, I met Marcel Vogel, a senior material scientist with IBM. He had pioneered scientific work in subtle energies and healing. At that time, I was "subtle energy ignorant." Marcel encouraged a 9-month study via rare books, as well as interviews with psychics, healers and energy researchers.

Marcel had an advanced research lab. His method of teaching was to show an effect and then see if the results and the implications were understood. In one of his early experiments, Marcel pulsed energy across the lab through a hand-held quartz transducer to an instrument that recorded the energy transfer on an oscilloscope.

A bright spot appeared on the screen each time the process was repeated. This basic experiment demonstrated that people can transmit energy through space to a distant point.

Reality Principle #3: Love-based intention facilitates healing.

A jeweler made me a similar transducer, a small four-sided square prism, 1.5 inches long, ending in a pyramid on one end and flat on the other end.

Marcel had arranged for me to meet and interview a Dallas psychic named Kay. When I arrived for the interview, she called in her neighbor, a nurse experiencing deafness in her right ear.

My transducer was in my pocket, but no one else was aware of its existence. To my surprise, Kay asked me to use my transducer to heal her friend's hearing.

I held the transducer with the tip touching the ear of the nurse and projected the thought of transmitting love and wellbeing to her. Within seconds the nurse stood up, smiled broadly, and started sobbing because she could hear again. This was my first healing experience.

Reality Principle #4: Use the Creator's Divine Love in all that you do to avoid transmitting limited love energy to recipients.

At O'Hare Airport, a woman in front of me suddenly fainted and collapsed on the terminal floor. Intuitively, I quickly placed the tip of my transducer at the juncture of her collar bone and sternum with the intention of love and wellbeing for her. Her eyes popped open and she said that she felt energy surging through her body.

She then asked how she had been revived so rapidly. I told her her body needed charging and balancing. She smiled knowingly and revealed that she was a professor at Palmer Chiropractic College in Bettendorf, Iowa. She invited me to visit her clinic to assist her with some difficult patients.

When Marcel Vogel was told about the encounter with the chiropractic doctor, he smiled, reached into his pocket and handed me a large quartz transducer which he had personally cut for me. It was about 5 inches long, four-sided, ending in a pyramidal shape on both ends. He told me that he had seen the design in a dream and wanted to study its therapeutic use. When I asked how to use it, he told me to use my intuition.

A few weeks later a meeting was arranged at the chiropractic doctor's clinic with about ten people, each in extreme pain. None had been helped by the doctor's traditional chiropractic treatments.

My technique was to hold an intention of sending love energy through the transducer to the patient. The patient was asked to pulse out breath, release whatever was responsible for the pain, and then draw in more love energy to restore the body.

All the patients released their original pain, but a curious thing happened: the men were pain free, but the women experienced a new pain that moved down their legs.

The next evening, believing that the effect was from a surface electrostatic energy discharge, the doctor asked women patients to remove pantyhose and put on cotton hospital gowns.

This corrected the moving pain problem, but did not explain why the pain suddenly appeared and moved down their legs.

Marcel began a weekend series of programs to train physicians and to discuss his subtle energy experiments. We described the female leg pain to the group, but no one could explain the effect.

Not long after, a physician working with me observed the issue with women patients and suggested using the Creator's love (Divine Love) rather than my personal love energy in the healing service.

I was amazed when, using the Creator's love, the traveling leg pain that the women had previously experienced did not materialize. We realized that my definition of love had been subject to my limited beliefs, which in turn had limited the energy.

Reality Principle #5: Energy follows thought.

Marcel Vogel held the original liquid crystal technology patent for digital time pieces. During a training session, we watched a split screen video from a lab experiment that he had prepared using his Zeiss microscope with an attached video system.

On the left, an amorphous liquid crystal exhibited a bland gray color. Then, when Marcel applied electricity to the liquid crystal, a thick dark outline of a block numeral appeared, followed by a light flash, then the area filled in, becoming a solid black numeral.

The right hand video showed a sample drop of blood from a person who had cancer. It had a ragged outline and colored blotches, as viewed through the microscope.

When Marcel focused his intention and pulsed love to the blood sample, the outline became a smooth, thick-lined oval. We saw a flash of light, and the sample changed composition, now appearing healthy on the video display.

When we form an intention and direct that thought to someone or something in a loving manner, Divine Love interacts with the intention and creates an effect. Marcel introduced this reality principle at almost every public meeting.

Reality Principle #6: Directed thought energy is not limited by distance.

With the help of a doctor in San Jose, California, Marcel conducted an experiment using a live philodendron plant. When the philodendron was connected to a Wheatstone bridge and lie detector-type electronics for recording any electromagnetic energy responses, the plant showed a straight line output.

Marcel left on a trip to India. At a predetermined time in India, Marcel focused on that faraway philodendron plant and sent it the thought of love. The plant responded immediately with a long smooth sine wave output.

Marcel next projected the thought of harming the plant. The recording device showed many high amplitude, saw tooth effects. This demonstrated again that intention can transcend distance.

Reality Principle #7: Always ask recipients if they want to be healed and are willing to take responsibility for their lives.

C. Norman Shealy, MD, operated a pain clinic in Springfield, Missouri, and often applied electro-stimulation with his Transcutaneous Electrical Nerve Stimulator (TENS) to patients. Dr. Shealy invited me to try helping some chronic pain patients.

Although many recipients were in severe pain and wanted relief, the healing service did not reduce pain in anyone, even though the

Creator's Love had been utilized. They were not *owning* the healing process!

A few days later the answer to the problem revealed itself. Once I began asking recipients at other locations if they WANTED to be healed, AND if they were willing to make the life changes needed to stay well, their healings became more successful.

Reality Principle #8: Industrial magnetic fields can harm us.

A TV technician suffering from intense stomach pain worked on TV sets with the protective shields removed. His subtle energy was adversely affected by his exposure to television magnetic fields. Resetting his energy fields eliminated the stomach pain.

I began taking a small electric motor to my workshops to demonstrate how even limited exposure to severe magnetic fields can throw the body out of balance.

Reality Principle #9: Acceptance of Divine Love deepens after healing.

A mother brought her 16-year-old daughter, a hemophiliac, to a doctor I was working with. The slightest cut would cause this young girl to bleed profusely, often requiring hospitalization.

At home after the healing, the girl intentionally cut her palm with a steak knife to see what would happen. She bled slightly, but then the wound clotted. There was no known "fix" for hemophilia.

Reality Principle #10: Not everyone accepts wellness.

Another case involved a 15-year-old deaf girl, a full-time resident at a Pittsburgh-area school for the deaf. Using a writing tablet to communicate, the girl wrote that she wanted her hearing restored.

A doctor and I performed the healing service using written communication; intuitively, we knew that the healing was complete, but that the girl was resisting. We told her she could hear if she gave herself permission to hear.

She replied in writing that she still could not hear. We wrote that she was loved and asked why she did not want to hear. She made no response.

When asked again, she grabbed the pad from my hand and wrote angrily that she had been in the deaf institution since she was a small child, and did not want to have to readjust to her family and the outside world. We reminded the girl that she could hear when she gave herself permission to do so. We had done all we could in her case.

It is important to remember that even when healing is offered with good intentions, it is the recipient's decision whether to accept it.

Reality Principle #11: Spiritual healing does not require physical instruments or an elaborate ceremony.

A physician asked me to sit in on the patient interview of a distressed mother and her 6-year-old son, who had been vomiting every half hour. We knew the boy had overheard his parents arguing and discussing divorce, and he had concluded he was the cause of the discord.

When the mother saw me take the transducer out of my pocket, she screamed that she would not allow me to use any device. I then placed the transducer on a table, out of the way.

As the boy climbed onto my lap, I smiled and asked if he knew that God loved him. When he responded positively, I asked him to just let go of his worry for Mommy and Daddy and let God take care of everything. He took a deep breath. As he let out his breath, all his energetic emotions released and the spasms and retching stopped.

My belief is that Divine Love was the effective intervention in this case; the intent of either the Spiritual Healer or the client can be used to produce healing effects. When we align our intention with the Creator's will, the best results are obtained; no tools or instruments are needed.

Reality Principle #12: Healing rates vary. Wait a suitable time before measuring results.

A woman diagnosed with terminal lung cancer asked for healing. Afterwards, we suggested she wait 10 days before going to a different doctor and hospital for a full medical workup; we knew that her current doctors would not expect her to be cancer-free. When she went to an out-of-state hospital all tests revealed that her cancer was completely gone.

In another case, I was interviewed on a television program about spiritual healing. After the interview, a woman called asking help for her husband who was scheduled for a quadruple heart bypass. He had been a WW2 navy corpsman on the first medical team to enter Nagasaki after the atomic bomb.

My intuition enabled me to determine that this man's heart chakra was closed down and the energy fields in his heart area were collapsed.

He desperately wanted the healing so we proceeded.

The client was told that he needed about 10 days for the healing to complete. When he returned home, he received a call from the hospital moving his surgery date to ten days later because of holiday personnel shortages. Coincidence?

After the 10 days, he insisted on having a pre-op workup. The tests showed absolutely nothing wrong with his heart. The puzzled staff canceled the planned surgery and he and his wife left the hospital.

The miracles exemplified by these two cases confirm that we should continually challenge our theories about health, illness and healing.

Reality Principle #13: Do only one healing on a recipient per day to allow for recovery.

During a seminar at a mountain retreat, Marcel Vogel divided the participants into two groups to work in two clearings separated by about 200 feet of dense pine forest. I would lecture one group and Marcel would simultaneously lecture the other group Our plan was to switch the groups three times, so they could hear three different lectures.

What transpired was totally unexpected. Each participant in my group asked for and received an individual healing as part of the lecture. The same request was made in Marcel's group.

After the first lecture, the groups switched. Neither Marcel nor I knew that each other's group had received individual healings during that first lecture.

At both second lectures, participants again asked for healings, presumably for different problems.

When the second lecture ended, the groups were expected to switch a third time for the final lecture. When no one showed up in either clearing, Marcel and I entered the woods in search of our groups. We met halfway and found all of the participants sitting or lying down, each exhausted from receiving two successive healings.

➢ *All participants had incorrectly assumed that they could increase their healing with concurrent healing sessions.*

Marcel and I recognized this as a major teaching. We both had used Divine Love in the healings rather than our own energy; our procedures were the same. We were aware that the people served were releasing some deep issues and experiencing corrections in their bodies. We also knew that people require several hours to adjust to a single healing.

Therefore, conducting a second healing before the effects from the first healing had totally "settled in" caused their body energy charges to drop, leaving the people extremely fatigued.

This experience also provided insight into the importance of deep breathing as a way to recharge the bioenergy fields. Deep breathing immediately following a healing was found to help people recover more quickly.

Development of The Divine Love Healing Process

Since the late 1980s, I have taught healing with Divine Love without instruments to facilitate healing and have experimented extensively with various ways to conduct more effective healings. I eventually developed a method for people to interact with the Creator using a statement I refer to as a *Petition*.

A petition contains reference to one's internal spirit, Divine Love, a statement of what is desired, and a statement to defer to the Creator's will. Changes occur over time, sometimes rapidly and sometimes slowly, according to the will of the Creator and the ability of the recipient's system to stabilize as he or she experiences energy changes.

The Future

In recent years, medical schools have included one or more courses on spirituality designed for medical students to develop more compassion and understanding of their devout patients.

However, these courses do not integrate spiritual healing with medicine. The integration of our Divine Love healing process, the Advanced Protocol, has not been integrated with modern medicine for reasons already stated.

Some medical professionals are now realizing that with the appearance of more sudden devastating illnesses, many of which cannot be treated medically, perhaps more spiritual solutions need to be implemented. Throughout the world there is deterioration in the spiritual, the mental, and the physical health of the general population.

Suffering continues to increase in parts of the world, often resulting from the unavailability of potable water and supplies of nutritious foods. Such conditions cannot be corrected without changing the focus of society from materialism to a spiritually guided life where the world's people learn to love as the Creator intended us to love.

CHAPTER 4

ATTAIN THE MIRACLE OF
DIVINE LOVE HEALING IN YOUR LIFE

In this and successive chapters, you will see *Custom Petitions* that should be used *exactly as presented* for people who have not been exposed to our Advanced Protocol. All of the Petition symptoms in this book can be used directly in the Advanced Protocol.

➢ *To help you correctly apply the Petitions presented, we have included after each of the Petitions, a **Statement of Use** which indicates how to use each Petition.*

The six topics in this chapter will help you attain your own miracle of healing with Divine Love; apply the topics as they relate to you.

Topic One: ACCORDING TO THE CREATOR'S WILL

This is the first and most important healing principle to recognize.

For self healing, some people use their own definition of love and many exclude the Creator. This produces inconsistent results as people try to impose their wills rather than being guided by the Creator.

Since 2009, every one of our petitions ends with "according to the Creator's will." This is done for two reasons:

First, we must recognize that the Creator is in charge of healing, not us. This means an individual cannot manipulate the Divine Love Petitions. Second, whether a petition is accepted or not is entirely up to the Creator.

When the Creator APPROVES a Healing Statement or Custom Petition that has been said aloud, Divine Love energy is activated and spiritual healing begins. Then, people may feel Divine Love energy moving in their body, or they may feel a reduction in their symptom.

If the Creator *denies* a petition, Divine Love does not flow, and the person continues to experience the symptom.

Just because a person believes in the Creator does not assure that the Creator will approve a healing request. The Creator takes into account one's entire life.

Asking the Creator for *forgiveness* for any bad behavior and expressing *gratitude* to the Creator may result in the Creator's approval of your petition.

Forgiveness has two components:

1. You forgive someone for something done to you.

2. You forgive yourself for something you have done to yourself or others.

You must include both components if you want to be completely forgiven by the Creator.

Statement of Use

Custom Petitions: Include the phrase "according to the Creator's will" at the end.

Advanced Protocol: The phrase is included in the Protocol; use the Protocol as given.

Topic Two: CHARGING AND BALANCING THE BODY

Charging and balancing constitute the second most important healing principle.

When someone is stressed, their body tries to heal naturally, but cannot because the body cannot take in energy fast enough or in the right amount to meet the healing demands.

Think of the body as a human battery that requires charging to function properly. In the context of energy healing, "charging" the body means that an individual is processing energy *into*, rather than *out,* of the body.

If a person has a very low energy level this condition is called "not being fully charged." If you are experiencing fatigue, mild dizziness, and have difficulty concentrating on what you are doing, it is likely that your body is at too low a charge.

The body may be charged with devices, with deep breathing, or with Petitions. When you work with Divine Love correctly, you quickly learn that Divine Love will fully charge the body.

"Balancing the body" is also important since the body can be charged, but not balanced. The body should be mentally, emotionally and physically stable, thus necessitating the need for balancing.

A state of *unbalance* may be seen in people who favor one side of their body over the other. If a person is fully balanced and is not experiencing an illness, the left and right sides of the body should function equally well.

The body is composed of multiple interlaced energy fields. When these fields are operating properly with respect to each other, the body is balanced. When the body is not balanced, the energy fields can create pressure in the system, causing localized pain and short-circuiting nerves. This is the beginning of inflammation which can increase and become life-threatening.

When a collapsed wrinkled balloon is inflated, all wrinkles expand and disappear as it assumes its intended shape.

When we utilize Divine Love to energetically charge and balance the body, the same thing happens. The body assumes its proper shape and functionality and the pain and the short circuiting of nerves begins to decrease.

When I worked in stressful environments, I used a petition technique to charge and balance my system. Many of my coworkers would be out of balance, which would adversely affect their health, their attitudes, and the ability to think clearly.

Use the Charging and Balancing Petition below for an immediate response.

As you say this petition aloud, the sound of your voice is transmitted to every cell in your body. Each cell then accepts the Divine Love energy needed.

CHARGING AND BALANCING PETITION

Say aloud:

"With my spirit I accept Divine Love continuously throughout my entire being. I ask that the Creator send Divine Love continuously throughout my entire being and charge and balance my entire system according to the Creator's will."

Draw in breath, close your mouth and pulse your breath lightly through your nose as if clearing your sinus. This frees the Petition in space to act on your system.

Statement of Use

Custom Petitions: Use the above Petition anytime exactly as given.

Advanced Protocol: Charging and balancing is accommodated in the Protocol. Anytime you want a quick energy boost, use the Charging and Balancing Petition exactly as given.

Charging and Balancing is necessary to your wellness because it aligns you with the Creator.

➢   *Before you interact with the Creator to ask questions, charge and balance your body completely so that you are fully functioning and able to receive accurate answers to your questions.*

If you are out of balance when you ask questions of the Creator or your Angels, you may get a response that you do not understand or cannot apply. This occurs because you are listening through energy filters that distort truth. Thus, when your system is not in alignment with the Creator, it is common to misunderstand the guidance you receive.

When you are in balance, you are aligned with the Creator and get accurate answers to your questions. You may then refine your questions to assure that you truly understand the guidance.

Topic Three: ASKING THE CREATOR FOR HELP

Most societies throughout the world have deep cultural traditions, generally based on historical belief systems and experiences.

However, because some information handed down over time is less accurate today, it may be misused or misinterpreted. This can lead to an intolerance for the beliefs and actions of others.

Being respectful of all religions and traditions means recognizing that there can be good in all, even though we might not fully understand the teachings.

In the midst of our current spiritual awakening, the spiritual truth is being made known. People can learn the spiritual and physical truth by paying close attention to their internal intuition which contains the spiritual truth. Then they can compare their truth with what they are being told by journalists, politicians, and others.

I believe there is a Divine Being I call the Creator. Think of the Creator as a Divine Spiritual Being who transcends all religions, all people, and all things throughout the universe. What I want you to understand is that you are not alone in this physical life.

➢ *We all have immediate access to Divine spiritual intelligence through the Creator and the Creator's Angels.*

The best healing results occur when we are "aligned" with the Creator and do not "own" the "misalignment" examples below:

➢ *Some people believe that the Creator has abandoned them.*

➢ *The Creator should be thought of as being neither male nor female. However, if women are brought up to fear men, the idea of a male Creator that can dominate women may be a source of subliminal fear.*

➢ *Some men believe that they have the right to dominate women.*

➢ *Some people believe that the power of the Creator is to be greatly feared, while also believing that the Creator loves them. Yet extreme fear blocks love, which is one of the reasons why some conflicted people have difficulty receiving Divine Love.*

➢ *As we release and heal from misalignment and we become aligned with the Creator, we learn that the Creator really does love us.*

We know that civilizations have suffered, and even ended, as a result of wars, famine, natural disasters, disease and human abuses. You may wonder why the Creator would allow any of these events.

The reality is that many of these conditions have been brought about because we humans have not taken care of each other and the earth in a loving manner. It is therefore vitally important for each of us to develop a close personal relationship with the Creator.

➤ *Again, please realize that it is the Creator of the universe, not you or I, who is in charge of providing healing.*

➤ *Thus, when we approach the Creator for help we should do so respectfully, without conditions, and without promises that we may be unable to keep.*

I believe that all life here and on other planets has been designed by the same Creator. We are all spiritual brothers and sisters; this applies across all countries on earth and throughout the universe.

As we learn to accept guidance from the Creator, we should apply that knowledge to help ourselves and our fellow man. The question then becomes: How do we get out of our own way to open ourselves up to Divine Guidance without fear of being manipulated or misled?

There are three things we can all do to help ourselves:

➢ *Ask the Creator for the healing you want in your own words, modeled after the following example called "Asking the Creator Petition."*

ASKING THE CREATOR PETITION

Say aloud:

"With my spirit I accept Divine Love continuously throughout my entire being. I ask that the Creator send Divine Love continuously throughout my entire being and heal my (insert your request) according to the Creator's Will."

Setting aside your personal opinions and beliefs about how things should be, allow the Creator to do the healing.

Observe your results. The proof is in what happens.

Statement of Use

Custom Petitions: Use the *Asking the Creator Petition.* The symptom = (specify what you want).

Advanced Protocol: Use the Protocol. Your Healing Statement symptom = (specify what you want); use the same symptom in both Healing statements.

Allow the Creator time to demonstrate your healing in a manner that you can recognize and accept. Divine Love healing by the Creator is a miracle whether based upon a simple request or by an all-inclusive process such as the Advanced Protocol.

You will be made aware if the Creator wants you to use the Advanced Protocol. Otherwise, ask for help and wait to see what happens.

Once you have asked the Creator for a healing, express in your own words your GRATITUDE for the healing. When you do this, you demonstrate your acceptance of the healing from the Creator, and help establish a bridge between the spiritual and the physical that allows your body to heal.

About Learning Your Truth

When I first began spiritual energy healing work, I wondered whether I was being contacted by a superior intelligence rather than the Creator, or whether I was being manipulated telepathically.

Learning how to recognize the truth takes time. What I finally realized was that information coming in *was to be honored, but not necessarily accepted.* I had to determine how best to ask questions that would produce answers I could understand and apply.

It would have been easy to believe everything I had been told, but had I done so, I would have failed because the information could include several possible interpretations and options.

For example, suppose you had cancer and had just completed a spiritual healing with Divine Love to eliminate the cancer. Five days later you ask the Creator: "Is my cancer healed?"

The answer is "Yes," but a blood test later that day still shows cancer markers. Obviously, something isn't right. The Creator doesn't lie or purposely mislead, so you need to ask a more specific question: "Is my cancer healed in *my entire system*?"

The answer this time is "No," so now you wonder what changed. What you learned with the second question is that the healing is not yet complete.

➢   *Healing is always done first in your spiritual self, then the physical body responds.*

The original "Yes" answer referred to the healing of your spiritual self.

Are You Talking to the Creator?

Nothing prevents us from talking to the Creator. Sometimes people question the reality of contact because we have been taught that "voices heard in the head" are not to be trusted. Remember: If you charge and balance your body before you dialog with the Creator, you will receive accurate information. Trust that the Creator wants the very best for us and will not mislead or harm us.

If you are having problems in your life that you do not understand, or if you are trying to use the Advanced Protocol and not getting results then:

➤   *In your own words, ask the Creator to explain what is wrong and what you need to do.*

Statement of Use

Asking a question is not a petition. If you are using the Advanced Protocol or Custom

Petitions with no improvement within a few days, use the Charging and Balancing Petition, then ask the Creator for guidance.

Once you ask the Creator your question, sit quietly until you can hear a soft voice "within" with an answer. When you get a response, ask more questions to be sure that you understand the message.

Sometimes people are told to use the Advanced Protocol to correct a specific symptom; other times, people are led to other solutions. If you have never seen or used the Advanced Protocol, the Creator will help you according to the Creator's will.

Do You Evaluate the Guidance Received?

The first answer may not be the only or best solution for you, so take the time to examine the words you hear and understand exactly what they mean for you at this time. Ask more questions until you are satisfied that you truly understand what instruction has been given.

Be assured, you are loved and are not being manipulated or harmed. If you accept Divine Love within yourself, then you can release untruths and symptoms.

Topic Four: CORRECTING UNLOVINGNESS

There is a wonderful energy field in the universe that we call the "Creator's Divine Love." This energy field is in a neutral state and stands ready to help heal spiritual, mental, and physical problems. If you correctly apply the healing techniques that we have introduced, most people achieve amazing healing results.

Your health improvements should be complete and lasting, provided that you are not operating negatively towards yourself, others, and the world in general. If you ARE in a negative state, then it may become necessary for you to release such behavior BEFORE you can heal.

Increased chaos throughout the world has caused people to become polarized and/or paralyzed by their beliefs. Unloving, firmly held negative or limited belief systems can slow,

73

block, or stop healing; people operating with a loving nature usually get excellent results.

Do You Understand Energy Flow?

Earlier, we discussed the importance of Charging and Balancing the body. Let me share the following word picture as an example of energy flow.

Consider a 5 gallon bucket filled with water. If you punch a 1 inch diameter hole in the bottom of the bucket you would expect all the water to run out of the bucket.

However, if someone is pouring sufficient water into the top of the bucket fast enough, despite the hole in the bottom, the bucket would appear to stay full.

In terms of your body, you are the bucket. The water is a stream of energy inside you; like the water in the bucket above, that energy needs to be constantly replenished. When energy runs out of your body, the result may be extreme fatigue, headache, brain fog, or aches and pains.

When this happens, your body struggles to compensate to preserve your energetic balance.

During the day you constantly receive energy from everywhere (putting water into the bucket). If that energy is *good* energy there is no problem. But if the incoming energy is *bad* (negative thought energy, for example), your body reacts to that negative energy. Those negative thoughts are examples of unlovingness.

Until you release negative energy (such as anger, fear, and other pent-up negativity), those negative energies can eventually overcome your system and you become out of balance energetically. When that happens, illnesses contained in your cellular structure that had been neutral, can now become active; you can become ill with a variety of symptoms!

The obvious solution is to put your body back into good energetic balance by allowing the Creator and Divine Love to charge and re-balance your system, eliminating the *bad* energy causing your illness. Remember this:

➢   *Your negative thinking and negative behaviors continue to put bad energy into your system; both represent unlovingness.*

When your immune system is overwhelmed with negativity, you may experience organ or immune system failure. Unlovingness may include combinations of the topics described below as well as any other negative thoughts, words, or deeds developed either in this life or inherited.

How can one become a "loving person" rather than an *unloving* person filled with hate, fear, doubt, uncertainty, or a lack of love for oneself or others? Simply "let go" of your unlovingness.
I will explain how to clear the negative energy effects of all these issues from your system even though you may not know which ones apply to you. We need to become aware of the key unlovingness issues.

Unlovingness Issues

Each of the seven topics below reflects key unlovingness issues we can eliminate from within ourselves to achieve improved health. Any of these issues can contribute to declining health.

Let's examine the issues first and then we will discuss clearing them.

1. Holding on to anger, hatred, or disdain for oneself or others.

Holding on to negative emotions often produces incomplete healing results. If a person uses the Advanced Protocol to correct a pain symptom, but has retained anger, hatred, or judgmental behavior that blocks them from healing, they must take action to release the energy blocks.

When you are distressed about your job, your health, or your government, and you articulate your opinion in a disparaging manner, you add more negative energy to your emotional energy blocks. And, because your thoughts, words or deeds are unloving, your healing eventually stops.

Deep-seated anger often results from a broken relationship, divorce, and/or physical and mental abuse. Intellectually, one might falsely convince oneself that any such anger has diminished, and that they must have success-fully forgiven the offender.

But anger does not diminish! Instead, that anger becomes a damaging negative energy field that can be activated by any number of life events. Thus, suppressed anger AND other unloving emotions deceive us because we do not recognize the EFFECTS they may have.

2. *Trying to force change in someone's behavior.*

Someone may believe that through their loving patience and guidance, he or she can change the behavior of another.

However, psychologists tell us that the only behavior we can change is our own. For example, if people marry with the expectation that over time their partner will change a behavior, both parties can become discontented.

Attempts to force change nearly always produce animosity and block communication.

3. *Confusion because of disinformation in the media.*

It is challenging to determine the truth by watching television, reading newspapers, or listening to commentators. Each source can have an agenda and competes for your agreement and support.

Friends and some family members may become polarized or even ostracized because of political, social, or religious disagreements. We each believe that we are "right" based upon our own "mental truths." This can create subconscious turmoil.

However, please understand that mental truth is not the same as spiritual truth.

4. *Spiritual Confusion.*

When people pray or ask for help from the Creator, they will receive guidance, but they *must* ask. And when they do ask, they need to understand that the answers coming to them are from a perfect spiritual environment.

Since our earthly life is imperfect, it is up to us to note, and eliminate, any discrepancies between the true spiritual guidance given and our current limited beliefs.

This corrective action brings us to a state of *being at one with the Divine*, as explained in my book BEING AT ONE WITH THE DIVINE.

Much too often, people reject spiritual guidance when:

➢ *It does not conform to their idea of what they believe they want or need.*

➢ *They do not believe that they are able to communicate directly with the Creator.*

➢ *They think the Creator is trying to control them.*

➢ *They do not like the spiritual guidance given to them by the Creator.*

We need to trust that our spiritual guidance is accurate and that it comes directly from the Creator or through Angels assigned to help us.

5. *Our mental resistance and limiting beliefs.*

Most of us as adults have experienced situations where we have been injured emotionally or physically, or both. This can either cause us to lose our self confidence and develop a submissive personality, or to develop mental toughness and resistance to change.

If we are unwilling to accept positive change, or cannot recognize the need for change, we retain our current limiting beliefs. For example, I have helped many people recover from cancer using our spiritual healing system. Yet others were not successful because they continued to hold onto false beliefs.

Believing that they cannot be helped is common among people who are mentally depressed. This condition is correctable once they accept that they can change and be healed.

6. *As we age, our limiting beliefs become more firmly ingrained.*

We use these conscious or subconscious beliefs every day to make decisions. If these decisions are not in alignment with spiritual truths, the results we get are poor, whether we are talking about a healing system or everyday activities.

7. *Not accepting that a Divine Being is in charge.*

It is important to accept our origins from the Divine Creator, existing in whatever form you believe. Furthermore, from the spiritual world, the Creator bestows upon us the ability to think and create in our physical world.

When we align ourselves with the Divine, our actions result in successful endeavors and spiritual healing in a time frame designated by the Creator, not us. We should not try to bend the Creator's will to our will.

Correcting Unlovingness In Patients

I've had some interesting experiences working with psychiatrists, other physicians, and clients. When you read the accounts below, perhaps you can match the situations to one or more of the seven unlovingness topics covered in this chapter.

One patient believed she was possessed by evil spirits and repeatedly told this to family members. This client had expressed what she believed so often that her belief eventually locked into her body.

Another client said she was afraid of her husband, believing he was looking for an opportunity to kill her. When I helped her release that thought, it came out of her in frightening images that finally vanished.

A doctor believed that he had somehow been infected by a patient. He was concerned enough that he consulted another doctor who was able to release him from the negative energy that had in fact infected him. As this energy came out, it formed the image of a squealing pig running around the doctor's office. When I arrived and asked about the pig, I learned that the image had eventually dissolved.

Such events are given to us to help us understand that human beings can be influenced by what are called "thought forms." These energetic thought forms can be strong enough to affect human behavior.

A psychiatrist's patient, struggling for three years to complete her doctorate, became dysfunctional whenever she sat down to write her dissertation.

As the patient tuned into what was bothering her, we learned that her manipulative father had expected her to enter a completely different field, while she simply wanted to make her own choices.

After I helped her release the frustration as well as the underlying cause of her dysfunction (her father's disappointment), she went on to get her doctorate in her chosen field.

84

Criticism Is Also Unlovingness

Several clients have had a common issue: They were oversensitive to criticism, often becoming belligerent when angry with others. When asked why they reacted that way, they would say they did not know.

That was their "truth;" they were not able to tap into their subconscious to determine what was actually upsetting them. Once put in touch with their issues and learning how to release them, they began to function normally and think rationally.

Evolution to Correct Unlovingness Issues

Before offering solutions to the preceding seven unloving issues, I would like to clear up any misunderstandings about the books published to date. My book BEING AT ONE WITH THE DIVINE offers a blueprint for how to change behavior and become one with the Creator. In that book, people are given an introduction to Lovingness Petitions, which preceded the original At

Oneness Healing System. Many readers have told me how the book has changed their lives.

The book DIVINE LOVE SELF HEALING describes the full At Oneness Healing System, with examples on how to apply the At Oneness Healing System properly by proceeding *more slowly* with the process. People aligned with the Creator are able to use this healing system successfully.

It became evident that some people needed additional help. Supplemental guidance appears in the book DYNAMIC REALITIES AND DIVINE LOVE HEALING, which added more petitions to the At Oneness Healing System, becoming known as the AT ONENESS HEALING SYSTEM ADVANCED PROTOCOL. The book shows exactly how to build an Advanced Protocol.

Most people successfully use either the original At Oneness Healing System or the Advanced Protocol. Some may not get their desired results due to one or more of the seven unloving energies described above.

We have taught that the Creator and your internal Spirit control all healing. If a firmly held limited belief conflicts with the Creator's Divine Love, spiritual healing may be withheld until the individual is able to acknowledge and remove that limited belief.

The next section will show how to remedy this.

How to Release Your Unlovingness Issues

Since most symptoms are the result of our unlovingness, we will examine how to best heal unlovingness issues.

Let's say we have a symptom we will call *foot pain*. There are two steps:

1. Begin by saying aloud the CHARGING AND BALANCING PETITION:

"With my spirit, I accept Divine Love continuously, throughout my entire being. I ask that the Creator send Divine Love continuously throughout my entire being and charge and

balance my entire system according to the Creator's will."

Pulse your breath and breathe deeply for five minutes.

➤ *This Petition will automatically charge and energetically balance your entire system before you continue with Step 2.*

➤ *Do not skip this step or shorten the time line.*

2. Next, release any unlovingness related to your symptom (foot pain) without extensive analysis of your unlovingness issues are, with the following:

CUSTOM UNLOVINGNESS PETITION

Say aloud:

"With my spirit and Divine Love, I focus on all my unlovingness associated with my (foot pain) and ask the Creator to release and heal that unlovingness and my (foot pain) completely according to the Creator's will."

Pulse your breath once and continue to breathe deeply for 15 minutes. Ask the Creator once a day if you are completely healed in *both* your spirit and physical body. It may take several hours or days to complete the healing, depending upon your illness.

➢ *Either the CUSTOM UNLOVINGNESS PETITION or the Advanced Protocol removes any unlovingness associated with whatever single symptom you specify. To prevent a person from overtaxing their system this occurs gradually and keeps the body in balance by stopping and starting a healing. Since unlovingness can accumulate over months or years, be patient; it takes time to clear your body.*

Statement of Use

Custom Petition: Use the CHARGING AND BALANCING PETITION followed by the CUSTOM UNLOVINGNESS PETITION described above exactly as given to heal ONE symptom (such as foot pain) and all the unlovingness blocks associated with that pain.

Advanced Protocol: Use the Advanced Protocol because all unlovingness energy related to *foot pain* is automatically removed as part of the Protocol. Use the symptom *foot pain* in both Healing Statements as described in the video, THE ADVANCED PROTOCOL AND HEALING STATEMENT TRAINING VIDEO.

Go Slowly

Modifying the above CUSTOM UNLOVINGNESS PETITION to eliminate ALL unlovingness in your entire body in one petition, at one time, is NOT recommended because the simultaneous healing of multiple unlovingness issues will make you overly fatigued.

While this CUSTOM UNLOVINGNESS PETITION affords a person the opportunity to use the Petition to clear a symptom, it does not contain all the features built into the Advanced Protocol. Remember to do deep breathing to better oxygenate your system because it speeds healing.

Topic Five: THE IMPORTANCE OF CORRECT BREATHING

The *Four-Cycle Deep Breathing Technique* has 4 steps:

Step 1-Breathe in slowly through your nose until your lungs are full.

Step 2-Hold your breath for 5 seconds.

Step 3-Breathe out slowly through the nose until your lungs feel completely empty.

Step 4-Do not breathe in again for 5 seconds.

Then repeat your Four-Cycle Breathing for 15 minutes. This is one session. Complete at least *four* sessions during the day.

Four-Cycle breathing accomplishes 4 objectives:

1.When you breathe in deeply and slowly, your cells have more oxygen available.

2. Holding breath in Step 2 of the Four-Cycle Breathing Technique transfers more oxygen into the lungs and from there into your bloodstream.

3. Breathing out slowly assures that your system has time to energetically process whatever is

being corrected by the Creator and Divine Love, and it helps remove old released energy.

4. Withholding breath in Step 4 of the Four-Cycle Breathing Technique allows discarded *bad* energy to completely leave the body during each completed cycle of Four-Cycle Breathing.

Why bother doing deep breathing? The best healing for cells occurs when blood oxygen is maintained between 90% and 100%.

➤   *DEEP BREATHING is necessary for success!*

➤   *If you do not maintain adequate blood oxygenation, HEALING STOPS until the body re-oxygenates. Healing may also continue at a reduced rate.*

If you have multiple health conditions, or are a shallow breather, oxygen levels may be in the range of 80% to 89%. This oxygen range will maintain your current condition, but will not significantly help accelerate your healing.

The Advanced Protocol energetically helps to stabilize your oxygen levels according to the Creator's will. However, you need to do your part by making up the difference through deep breathing.

During development of the Advanced Protocol, we learned that some people were just too ill to do any deep breathing. If you are very ill, cannot do deep breathing, or consistently experience less than 90% oxygen throughout the day, we suggest you contact your physician to discuss obtaining a portable oxygen device.

For those who have no access to an oxygen machine, we added a petition to provide the energetic equivalent of oxygen, helping people heal according to the Creator's will. However, if you can breathe unassisted, it is your obligation to do deep breathing as your commitment to working with the Creator to achieve wellness.

Everyone can make rapid advances in healing when they are able to increase their oxygen levels. To evaluate your need for oxygen, an inexpensive finger oxygen meter will display your oxygen levels. We should know what our oxygen levels are as we heal.

Observed Breathing Problems

Being Unaware

People are often unaware of both what is healing in their bodies at any point during the day and how fast that healing is taking place.

Obviously, if you have been in pain and the pain is going away while you're doing the Advanced Protocol with deep breathing, you know that you're moving in the right direction with regard to how many sessions of Four-Cycle Breathing Technique are necessary. Do not assume because a pain has temporarily departed that you are completely healed. Always ask the Creator if you are completely healed in your spiritual self and in your physical body before changing to a new symptom.

People ask if they can get by with only 15 minutes of deep breathing. They say they do not have time to do more. My response is generally the same, which is to ask how quickly they want to heal. The more deep breathing sessions done consistently throughout the day, the better.

If, you are a perfectly healthy person healing the pain from a bumped elbow, for example, and using the Advanced Protocol, you can generally get by with fewer breathing sessions, each five minutes long.

However, if you have a major disease or multiple diseases, it should be obvious that only one symptom at a time is going to heal. You may need to do extensive breathing sessions to get a proper result, which you can recognize if it is a physical or emotional feeling. If it is not, then you need to learn how to test for completed breathing, which is synonymous with a test for a symptom being healed. Simply ask the Creator.

Breathing Too Fast

It's best to breathe slowly and deeply to avoid becoming lightheaded. If you do become a bit lightheaded, simply pulse your breath with the intention of clearing the lightheadedness.

Not Maintaining the Four-Cycle Breathing Technique

For people with life-threatening diseases, it is recommended to spend as much time as needed each day doing deep breathing. This may seem like a lot of concentrated breathing effort, but most people will invest the necessary time to become well.

You Need to Be Aware of What Your Body Is Telling You

Sometimes your system needs more oxygen to physically heal a particular group of cells, such as damaged organs. If you stop doing deep breathing when it is most needed, *discomfort may result*. Overcome that discomfort by increasing the number of Four-Cycle Breathing sessions.

We always suggest doing deep breathing in multiple *sessions*. A session can be 5 to 15 minutes long. If you complete at least four deep breathing sessions a day, you will have a total of 20 to 60 minutes of deep breathing per day.

For faster results, do *more* deep breathing sessions per day. Some people set timers or use reminder notes to help remember their deep breathing sessions. Do deep breathing properly and you should see major improvements in your healing.

Please remember, we are teaching a healing process that is spiritual, not mental. Spiritual healing depends upon your developing a positive relationship with the Creator of the universe. If you do not honor that connection, you may not get results.

When you honor the connection to the Creator, your results are also determined by your willingness to do self-healing work. Stick with it until you are well, or until you are guided to do otherwise by the Creator.

➢ *Working with Divine Love and the Advanced Protocol should develop into a way of life, dealing with all spiritual, mental, and physical issues as they arise.*

Statement Of Use

After using a Custom Petition or the Advanced Protocol, do the Four-Cycle Deep Breathing Technique until results are achieved. When in doubt about how long it takes, ask the Creator; other things may need to be healed first.

Topic Six: ALL ABOUT SYMPTOMS

There are several important issues regarding the use of symptoms. We define a symptom as something that you experience either emotionally or physically.

➤ *Please do not use a medical diagnosis as a symptom unless that diagnosis has been confirmed by medical tests that do not have false positives. We have learned that if an incorrect diagnosis is used, no healing takes place because you asked for the wrong thing!*

Describing Symptoms

Over many years, we have experimented with how to best describe symptoms. We learned that when clients used a *single* symptom to describe their situation, they got better results more quickly than if they tried to use multiple symptoms. For example, if you have a *headache*, but also have *tingling in your feet*, and an *itchy patch* in your armpit, you want to identify the most important single symptom. You would probably pick "headache."

You do not need to know the underlying root cause of your symptom (the headache). If it is important for you to know the root cause, it will become known to you either through your intuition or through the Creator's guidance.

Protection Against Misuse

Suppose that *headache* is a single symptom, but that you also have an unidentified and unrelated life-threatening condition for which you have no presented symptoms. The healing mechanism protects you against that life-threatening event. Whether you ask the Creator for help using your own Customized Petition or using the Advanced Protocol, help is given.

➤ *If you have a life-threatening condition, whether known to you or not, the Creator will usually stabilize or heal that life-threatening condition BEFORE dealing with your stated symptom.*

You may not recognize when that Divine Love energy is being directed to that unknown condition because the healing takes place in the background. This is another reason why doing the Four-Cycle Breathing Technique is so important; the amount of oxygen needed to heal even that *unknown* condition is also unknown.

People sometimes believe nothing is happening when the symptom they are trying to clear remains. However, once your unknown life-threatening condition is stabilized, even if not completely healed, your specified symptom (*the headache*) will usually heal rapidly.

If you have multiple life-threatening conditions that you DO know about, but you are more interested in healing the headache, the same priority of healing will apply. And you should anticipate the need for more Four-Cycle Breathing Technique sessions.

Many people have multiple issues. If they exhibit too much *unlovingness,* or do the *breathing insufficiently*, or *specify simultaneous symptoms*, their spirit generally STOPS the healing. This prevents a person's system from going into a strained energy condition due to insufficient oxygen in the cells. (Remember when the students that Marcel Vogel and I were working with were found lying in the woods?)

Do Not Change Symptoms
Until The Healing Is Complete

Believing they have done something wrong when they do not get immediate results, people may change symptoms hoping for a better outcome.

However, if the first symptom is not healed completely, and you change to a new symptom, the current Petition stops working on Symptom 1 and switches to Symptom 2.

If you allow your second symptom to run to completion, Symptom 2 may be healed. All healing depends on the Creator's acceptance of your Custom Petition symptom or Advanced Protocol symptom.

Unless you have just had an accident, most conditions have existed in your system for some time. For example, someone may have been exposed to a toxin many years earlier; now it is manifesting as an illness that is overloading the immune system.

Do Not Specify Multiple Symptoms in Any Petition

The most difficult unintentional misuse of a Customized Petition or Advanced Protocol occurs when a person decides to lump several problems into one symptom. This starts a healing process to address all the symptoms *simultaneously*.

Now you realize that if you do not do the Four-Cycle Breathing Technique for long enough, or get enough oxygen, none of the symptoms will heal. Therefore, it is important:

➢ *To specify only ONE symptom in a Custom Petition or Advanced Protocol.*

➢ *To do the Four-Cycle Breathing Technique four sessions per day for 15 minutes or longer each session until healing is complete.*

➢ *To increase the number of Four-Cycle Breathing Technique sessions per day and/or increase the time for each session to heal a symptom more quickly.*

➢ *To ask the Creator to identify what may be impeding your progress and what type of corrective action is to be taken if you do not see healing within 10 days.*

➢ *To learn about all of our Divine Love testing techniques in the book DYNAMIC REALITIES AND DIVINE LOVE HEALING.*

Healing Petition Differences

Pop ups are thoughts/energy blocks that impede healing. Pop ups coexist in layers within energy fields; not all pop ups are directly associated with the symptom you are trying to heal.

Statement of Use

Custom Petitions: If something unexpected "pops up," it can put a strain on the body, and healing stops. If one does not have sufficient experience to recognize the problem, they can remain stuck.

Advanced Protocol; Multiple Petitions built into the Protocol account for unexpected *pop ups*, so your healing continues.

The book DYNAMIC REALITY AND DIVINE LOVE HEALING specifies one Healing Statement with multiple uses. Initially it is used just ONCE to address a single symptom. For successive uses, the same Healing Statement is used to address *pop-up symptoms* that may be stuck in your energy fields.

The book explains exactly how to use the Healing Statement correctly. People who want to more actively participate in their healing steps may prefer to implement the book version of the Advanced Protocol.

People less interested in details will find that the video, THE ADVANCED PROTOCOL AND HEALING STATEMENT TRAINING VIDEO, is easy to use, with no need to worry about the phenomenon called pop-up symptoms. Here is why:

➢ *As we continued to refine the Advanced Protocol, we constructed, tested, and then taught the protocol via online webinars. This Advanced Protocol consisted of TWO separate Healing Statements.*

➢ *Both Healing Statements are each said only one time, as demonstrated in the video.*

➢ *The first Healing Statement is used to specify and heal a single symptom.*

➢ *The second Healing Statement auto- matically heals all pop-up symptoms associated* with the first Healing Statement. (The second Healing Statement uses exactly the same symptom wording as used in the first Healing Statement.)

➢   When either Healing Statement senses an energy disturbance, the correct Healing Statement runs and the other Healing Statement suspends operation until the disturbance is corrected. Only one Healing Statement runs at a time.

I prefer the video-based system because it is easier to use and, as already stated, you do not have to keep track of pop ups; the two Healing Statements keep track for you. What you *must* do, however, is maintain your deep breathing.

When you are experiencing a pop-up symptom, just do deep breathing to release it. Sometimes, if you sense the presence of an uncomfortable emotional problem, you can speed up the pop-up release by literally giving yourself permission to heal. Additional information is provided in the book and in the video.

A Symptom Can Be Located
In Space Around the Body

The human body is a mass of unseen vibrating energy fields which do not end at the skin's surface. Energy fields oscillate outside the body.

As you breathe in, your energy fields contract to your skin's surface. As you breathe out, your energy fields expand several feet from the skin's surface.

In a healthy and energetically well-balanced individual, energy fields exist equidistant everywhere around the body, extending about 6 inches into space. If someone is unwell, however, their energy fields may be unstable and may project many feet from their physical body.

Although this phenomena is interesting, it does not adversely affect the body unless one is being constantly overwhelmed. When this occurs, the energy fields in space begin to collect unloving thoughts.

When one consistently uses a petition to release unwanted unloving thoughts, the external energy fields eventually clear, and usually remain clear, while expanding and contracting about 6 inches as one breathes.

However, when these external energy fields are not cleared, they begin to compress into our physical body and can take up residency at any place in or around the body. If these energy fields become dense enough, they actually interfere with cells; an illness that had previously been kept in check by the immune system may become activated.

Another example: If one has been thinking of something disturbing and then happens to be in a car accident, those disturbing thoughts can be imprinted into the body or into the external energy field upon impact.

An Energy Field Discovery

One day I was introduced to a woman who had been badly hurt in a car wreck. She had recovered from the physical damage, but her speech had become garbled and she did not form complete sentences.

I noticed that she was radiating energy from different places in the energy field outside of her body. While tracing those energy disturbances in space with my finger, I noticed that each one brought to my mind a short phrase. The fragmented thoughts were randomly scattered in space around her body. I recorded the phrases, but they made absolutely no sense.

I learned that just before the accident, she and her husband had had a verbal disagreement prior to her angrily driving off in her car. Considering those events, I arranged about a dozen of the phrases on a timeline based on the argument; we were able to see rudimentary thought forms of what she had been thinking.

This discovery explained why people in other difficult cases did not respond well to healing. The unloving thoughts that were stuck in the energy fields surrounding those patients were the root causes of their distress!

When energy healers work with people, they frequently are not aware that a symptom can be located in space. Since the introduction of the Advanced Protocol, it no longer matters if an underlying cause is located on the body, in the body, or in space around the body, because the Healing Statements used are all-inclusive and address the entire spirit, soul, mind, energetic fields, and physical body.

Do Not Rush a Healing

Be aware that Divine Love spiritual healing is not to be taken lightly. Some people mistakenly think that if they get a favorable symptom healing, they should immediately work on another symptom.

However, each symptom has its own healing rate and to see that effect fully developed in the body may take time. Be patient and give your body a chance to heal.

➤ *To make this point, I always ask clients if they would consider having brain surgery and knee surgery on the same day. And of course they would not. Think of your healing in the same terms, allowing your body to heal one symptom before transitioning to another symptom.*

"Some people want it to happen,
some wish it would happen,
others make it happen."

- Michael Jordan

"If we live in our oneness-heart,
we will feel the essence of all religions
which is the love of God. Forgiveness,
compassion, tolerance, brotherhood
and the feeling of oneness
are the signs of a true religion."

- Sri Chinmoy

CHAPTER 5

HEALING NEUROLOGICAL ISSUES

Brain Injuries

Brain injuries develop in a variety of ways, including Chronic Traumatic Encephalopathy (CTE), the progressive brain condition likely caused by repeated episodes of concussions. Using conventional medicine, some injuries may be treatable and some may not.

We have had positive brain healing experiences working with Divine Love. As people gain more experience working with Divine Love and the Creator, I suspect we will see many positive healing results for illnesses that could not be treated conventionally.

Other accident-based brain injuries can leave the injured person with reduced motor function.

Cancer of the brain appears as tumors; some tumors are operable but others are not. (We have experience with many types of cancer, but have only worked with one brain cancer patient; her cancer was healed.)

Another subtle injury occurs over a period of time when the brain is invaded by toxins, causing neural connections to fail. Both dementia and Alzheimer's are examples of how a disease can lead to progressive deterioration of the brain. With these, the brain no longer recognizes all the conditions happening within the body.

A simple example: A brain-healthy person with a bruised and swollen foot may choose to quickly and successfully treat any foot swelling with cold packs. In that person, the body sends the brain status signals, feedback to the brain.

The brain knows what the body needs for the body to heal. The brain may send a signal to move more or less fluid to an injury site to protect the site while it is healing.

However, for someone with a brain injury as a result of toxins attacking the brain, the injured foot may not respond to treatment in a reasonable time frame, or may not exhibit any improvement at all.

Someone may also have physical therapy to help the foot heal. The body would report healing status to the brain and the healthy brain would modify the instructions to the body based upon the body's state of recovery. The brain would eventually tell the body to reduce the amount of fluid causing the swelling.

In a person experiencing a *toxic brain injury*, the feedback signal provided to the brain from the body can be lost for any number of reasons, and then the brain does not receive feedback; the brain continues to send the command to maintain the swelling.

In addition, if a person experiences pain and swelling, neither the pain nor the swelling will necessarily go away when the neural circuits in the brain have been interrupted.

The Brain Healing Technique

An injury to my hand caused it to be swollen, stiff, painful, and slow to heal. When I asked the Creator what exactly needed to be done, I was surprised by the response.

I was told to use a particularly worded petition because a portion of my brain had been damaged by toxins and was no longer able to process certain feedback from my body. The *feedback* control would normally be able to recognize improvements and decrease the need for extreme swelling, stiffness and pain.

The Brain Healing Technique the Creator gave me is composed of two petitions:

1. The BRAIN HEALING PETITION
2. The BRAIN UNIFICATION PETITION

I was told that we can use the Brain Healing Technique when the body does not respond to healing within a reasonable amount of time. There are two steps to brain healing: Healing the brain first, and then healing the body and brain together.

Both healings can be done using either the Brain Healing Petition shown below, or by using the Advanced Protocol.

BRAIN HEALING PETITION

Say aloud,

"With my spirit I accept Divine Love continuously throughout my entire being. I ask the Creator to send Divine Love continuously throughout my entire being. I ask the Creator to heal my brain damage according to the Creator's will."

Remember to close your mouth, breathe in deeply and pulse your breath once to release the petition. Do deep breathing sessions and wait awhile. (Healing may take several minutes, hours or days depending upon the severity of the damage.)

Do not proceed further until you ask the Creator and are told that your brain is COMPLETELY healed in both your spirit AND physical body. DO NOT SKIP THE WAITING PERIOD, OR CHANGE TO ANOTHER PETITION WHILE THE BRAIN IS HEALING.

This Brain Healing Petition need only be said once. This Petition combines several essential functions into one petition:

➢ *"Accept Divine Love" is giving ourselves permission to continually accept Divine Love internally.*

➢ *Asking the Creator to send Divine Love throughout the entire body overcomes both the fear paralysis many people experience and whatever else may be blocking them.*

➢ *We ask the Creator to heal our brain damage, rather than trying to do it on our own.*

➤ *We include "according to the Creator's will" for the reasons stated in Chapter 4.*

This Petition is identical to the ASKING THE CREATOR PETITION format. Help yourself by using the BRAIN HEALING PETITION; observe what happens. When the Creator tells you that your brain is completely healed, you may implement the BRAIN UNIFICATION PETITION. Otherwise, wait awhile and re-ask the Creator.

I learned that people with a damaged brain need to reconnect signals from the brain to and from the body. The brain could initiate an action to say, move a limb, but until the brain is reconnected with the *entire body*, feedback from the body to the brain may be incomplete.

BRAIN UNIFICATION PETITION

Say aloud: *"With my spirit I accept Divine Love continuously throughout my entire being. I ask the Creator to send Divine Love continuously throughout my entire being. I ask the Creator to heal all connections to my brain according to the Creator's will."*

Close the mouth, inhale deeply, and pulse breath through the nose once. Do the above Petition only once.

Do deep breathing sessions and wait awhile. (Healing may take several minutes, hours or days depending upon the severity of the damage.)

Do not proceed further until you ask the Creator and are told that your BRAIN UNIFICATION PETITION has COMPLETELY healed in both your spirit and entire physical body.

DO NOT SKIP THE WAITING PERIOD, OR CHANGE TO ANOTHER PETITION WHILE THE BRAIN UNIFICATION PETITION IS HEALING.

This petition requires an explanation to absorb the multiple events taking place.

➢   *The "entire being" includes the spirit, soul, mind, and the etheric and physical bodies comprising the human system.*

➤ *When the brain is damaged, it may lose feedback connectivity with the rest of the body, which is "all connections to my brain."*

Statement of Use

Let's say you are trying to heal *back pain*, but nothing is happening.

Custom Petition: Say the BRAIN HEALING PETITION following the instructions exactly. Again, do not proceed further until you ask the Creator and are told that both your spirit *and* your physical body are completely healed.

Then say the BRAIN UNIFICATION PETITION exactly as described above. Again, do not proceed further until you ask the Creator and are told that both your spirit *and* your physical body are completely healed.

Next, put the *symptom* you want to heal *(back pain)* into your ASKING THE CREATOR PETITION and complete the desired healing.

Test for complete healing by asking the Creator, or by using one of the test methods described in the book DYNAMIC REALITIES AND DIVINE LOVE HEALING. Remember to continue deep breathing as the energy of Divine Love corrects the problem in the body.

Advanced Protocol: There are two petitions called Healing Statements which are used for symptom correction as described in the previously referenced Advanced Protocol video. The first Healing Statement is used for a symptom you want to correct. The second Healing Statement uses the same symptom wording to automatically correct only pop-ups associated with the specified symptom.

To heal the brain, use the same symptom (*brain damage*) in both Healing Statements.

After you ask the Creator and get confirmation that the brain is completely healed in spirit and in your physical body, you are ready to do the *BRAIN UNIFICATION PETITION*. Use the symptom (*all connections to my brain)* in both Healing Statements.

After you ask the Creator and get confirmation that *all connections to my brain* are completely healed in both spirit and your entire physical body, you are ready to heal your back pain.

Put the *symptom* you want to heal (back pain) into both Healing Statements. Remember to do deep breathing until the Advanced Protocol has finished.

Test for complete healing in both your spirit and in your entire physical body by asking the Creator, or by using one of the test methods described in the book DYNAMIC REALITIES AND DIVINE LOVE HEALING.

Results

For my problem hand, the results were truly amazing. I used the Advanced Protocol. When I did the BRAIN HEALING PETITION, I felt a strong vibration in my head that lasted about 20 minutes. Then I found that I could move my wrist without pain! The wrist and fingers were still stiff and there were some slight pain twinges when I first moved my hand. And then the pain was COMPLETELY gone!

I waited several days to see what would happen. When the other symptoms remained I did the BRAIN UNIFICATION PETITION. Surprisingly, I saw a reduction in hand stiffness, but because the swelling persisted, the next morning I used the Advanced Protocol to correct the stiffness. As I did the deep breathing throughout the day, the stiffness melted away and the swelling went down.

Application Opportunities

Ordinarily, unless people recognize their brain injuries, they would not know about a brain toxin, such as the one that had interfered with me. We usually learn about brain toxins when a family member has Alzheimer's or advanced dementia.

I have used the Advanced Protocol successfully with many people who had less severe brain injuries; three applications are described below.

1. During one of our 2017 spiritual research programs, we determined that people who had at least partial possession of their faculties could use the Advanced Protocol for both dementia and Alzheimer's and experience some improvement, if not total healing. Correcting brain damage in Alzheimer's and dementia clients should be considered a spiritual research healing program. It also requires close monitoring that is beyond the scope of this book.

In that research study, we used only the BRAIN HEALING PETITION; results were incomplete. However, we did see some improvement in those dementia clients who had greater possession of their faculties.

The measurement of Alzheimer's results was complicated by patient side effects from drugs given to suppress anxiety, as well as lack of access to patients in locked wards. We were dependent upon visiting family members, who did their best to report objectively, but lacked the training to evaluate progress.

2. Over the last 30 years, we have been able to help many patients with learning disabilities recover full use of their mental faculties. This group includes former drug addicts, people dysfunctional from toxins, and clients severely injured in accidents.

3. We have also helped correct some suspected or confirmed brain damage when that prevented some other *symptom* from healing, such as a pain or a disease.

Physical Therapy Techniques

Over the years I have sustained injuries in various parts of my body. Being a firm believer in good physical therapy, I like to integrate their teachings with my own techniques. Sometimes this results in accelerated healing. Recovery can be a collaborative effort between the physical therapist and Divine Love petitions.

Nerve Damage

Many people exhibit neurological malfunctions. These malfunctions may also affect other parts of the body. If this is happening to you, use a Healing Statement to correct the neurological problem first. Be patient because nerve damage healing rates are a function of age, physical condition, type of injury, and nerve health.

If you discover that nerve damage has restricted your healing, you need to start over and first release your unlovingness energy blockages. Then work toward correcting any nerve damage.

Be aware that nerves interacting elsewhere may affect the nerves in your injury. For example, you might have injured a back or chest muscle, but because the nerves flow through those muscles and go down the arm and into the hand, the pain appears in the hand.

➢ *Always remember to use petitions as needed to isolate all potential underlying causes of damage that restrict healing, not just at the physical injury site, but also for other energetic causes such as negative thoughts or crushed nerves.*

As you gain more experience with these concepts, you will notice a profound, more confident change in your outlook.

"When we are spiritually healthy, we realize that we exist beyond the physical and our life has a sense of meaning and purpose."

- Dr. Robyn L. Gobin

CHAPTER 6

BEHIND THE SCENES
OF
DIVINE LOVE HEALING

In previous books I explained how the Angel Teachers came to me once I committed myself to helping others. Many people cannot comprehend that the Creator's Angels are available to help us.

To evaluate the concept, I followed just three simple guidelines:

1. Whatever I Learned Had to Be Real and Applicable In Our Physical World.

Over the years, the Angels led me through a progression of increasingly difficult cases. As my understanding increased, more information was given.

One issue was how to know when a healing is complete. When the Angels would tell me that a healing had been accomplished, they meant that the healing was done in the spiritual realm, but not necessarily in the physical.

➢ *I learned that the healing energy had to cross the barrier from the spiritual kingdom to the physical kingdom.*

➢ *And that energy needed to be accepted into the body of the client.*

For example, Divine Love would flow to a client with the stated intention of healing a specified underlying cause of a physical complaint. However, since people often have limited thinking, emotional energy blockages can prevent or block Divine Love energy from entering their bodies.

Also, if an individual believes they aren't worthy of being healed, that thought becomes an energy block. That energy block may be strong enough to prevent healing.

I learned that when people truly desire healing, and are willing to take responsibility for themselves, and are also willing to correct the behavior that made them unwell, then they healed rapidly!

2. Whatever I Learned Had to Be Uncomplicated and Readily Demonstrable to Others.

Many of the healings that took place could not be explained by science or medicine.

Many illnesses had been considered incurable. And for those that were curable, most physicians did not expect to see clients become well in a matter of hours or days.

One feature of Divine Love is that not everyone responds at the same rate. And, some people are not helped at all.

Eventually I learned that there are two parts to our consciousness, which I call the *active* and the *subconscious.*

➢ *To eliminate all of our personal active and subconscious resistance to healing, we simply need to give ourselves permission to heal, which is done by accepting healing with Divine Love.*

The Acceptance Petition for a healing was first expressed by: *"With my spirit, I accept Divine Love throughout my entire being."*

The above short petition works very well. However, as we learned more about charging and balancing, it was evident that an energy boost would be needed to get results faster.

We expanded the above petition, renaming it the "Charging and Balancing Petition." It is repeated here from Chapter 4.

CHARGING AND BALANCING PETITION
Say aloud:

"With my spirit, I accept Divine Love continuously throughout my entire being. I ask that the Creator send Divine Love continuously throughout my being and charge and balance my entire system according to the Creator's will."

The Charging and Balancing Petition is recommended for use BEFORE, DURING, and AFTER any healing action or petition described in this book. The Charging and Balancing Petition indicates that the person stating the petition is surrendering themselves to the Creator's Divine guidance, overriding any active and subconscious resistance to healing.

The petition provides an immediate energy boost and resets balance of the body.

The petition also enables the Advanced Protocol to restart if necessary. Reasons for the Advanced Protocol to have stopped:

➢ Stoppage occurs when the body requires more oxygen to facilitate healing. This is rectified by doing deep breathing.

133

➤ *By stopping the flow of Divine Love you are encouraged to ask questions of the Creator to discover why Divine Love is not healing your symptom. This is a learning opportunity.*

➤ *Refusing to acknowledge the existence of unloving behavior once the Creator has identified it.*

➤ *Refusing to change unloving behavior.*

When you take corrective action to release unlovingness, the Advanced Protocol will resume.

Why do we resist healing when we are ill, suffering instead of using a proven healing system? Several reasons are:

Sometimes ill people believe they deserve to be punished.

People may subconsciously resist healing when they get more attention from their family or friends when they are unwell.

Sometimes, when people explore a new healing modality but do not get results, they simply give up, believing that they must remain ill. Of course that is not true; you can work with Divine Love to change any behavior, provided that it is permitted by the Creator.

➢ *When clients use the* Charging and Balancing Petition *healing rates increase rapidly.*

When people ask the Creator for a spiritual healing using The Advanced Protocol, all of the petitions associated with the Advanced Protocol operate as needed, and the healing is completed on the spiritual level.

➢ *When people give themselves permission for Divine Love energy to enter them, that healing energy permeates the physical body at a safe rate, energetically modifying cells and DNA; the physical body is healed at the cellular level.*

➢ *As resistance from fear and hate is finally eliminated, the body enters a state of energetic balance (oneness with the Creator) so that the healing can complete.*

➢   *This petition helps people rapidly break through their fear.*

3. Whatever Was Taught Could Do No Harm.

No client has ever been harmed with Divine Love. If the Creator sanctions healing, it is completed over time, provided the client abides by the principles presented in this book. When cases of extreme pain go away quickly, the clients gratefully accept this positive life change.

With many new medicines brought to market each year, inherent in each is the potential for harmful side effects. Yet, we should realize that no company can identify all potential chemical side reactions that can occur for any given medicine.

Some medicines are fully consumed with no residual effect. Yet, taken over time, some medicines become toxic and that toxicity may be greater when combined with what we eat, drink, breathe, or even absorb through the skin.

Although many medicines are flushed out of the body when their use is discontinued, we have seen cases where clients had old medicines in their systems that suddenly reacted with a new medicine.

As reported in my book DYNAMIC REALITIES AND DIVINE LOVE HEALING, people can use the Advanced Protocol to remove harmful side effects. We can be proactive and ask the Creator to protect us against side effects from any medicine we have taken or are about to take.

About Drug Overdoses

Drug overdoses everywhere have become so common that emergency workers are carrying Narcan to help reverse opioid overdose. While this intervention can prevent people from dying, the treatment does not correct or identify any of the underlying reasons for a drug addiction.

I decided in 2017 to offer our drug addiction healing methods to the general public. We ran a spiritual research program for people to break their addictions to drugs or alcohol, or both. That study was highly successful and taught us:

➤   *If a drug addicted person desired to rid themselves of their addiction and believed in the Creator, by using the Advanced Protocol they could break an addiction in a few hours, with no side effects, and, WITH NO PAIN, AND WITH NO WITHDRAWAL SYMPTOMS.*

➤   *If the drug addicted person did not believe in the Creator or was not fully committed to wanting relief from the addiction, their healing either did not happen or was prolonged for several days.*

➤   *When someone asks for help, they must be fully committed to changing their behavior. Only limited success was met by alcoholics who wanted to allow some "occasional, social" drinks and by other drug users who wanted to allow "occasional" recreational use.*

➢ Because of how state rehab programs are constructed in the United States, it is virtually impossible to introduce our healing process into those institutions. This is why we offered to the general public the free spiritual healing program for correcting addictions.

This was presented as a spiritual healing program under the direction of the Creator; each applicant was evaluated by the Creator. (For more information, visit our website: worldserviceinstitute.org and examine the "FREE Programs" tab.

Rehabilitation centers are welcome to incorporate the AT ONENESS HEALING SYSTEM ADVANCED PROTOCOL we offer along with their established regimens. This could accelerate recovery, break dependency on subsequent support meetings, and eliminate any tendencies to relapse.

Correcting Other Overdoses

Someone does not need to be in an addiction program to block a side effect. Perhaps you mistakenly took too much of a medicine and are experiencing disturbing side effects. This is a common problem, especially for some older people who do not carefully monitor their medicines. Get immediate relief with the following Petition:

OVERDOSE PETITION

"With my spirit I accept Divine Love continuously throughout my entire being. I ask that the Creator send Divine Love continuously throughout my entire being. I ask the Creator to neutralize any harmful side effects from my overdose according to the Creator's will."

You can use the Advanced Protocol for complex situations involving multiple medicines.

Importing Needed Spiritual Energy Medicine

There is also the situation where there is no access to the physical medicines needed to treat an illness. The Creator *may* help, on a limited basis. You might say this Petition:

SPIRITUAL ENERGY MEDICINE PETITION

Say aloud:

"With my spirit I accept Divine Love continuously throughout my entire being. I ask that the Creator send Divine Love continuously throughout my being. I ask the Creator to provide the energy of the medicine needed to heal me according to the Creator's will."

Remember to pulse your breath.

This is not a free substitute for getting needed medicine. It is meant to help you only on a temporary basis.

The words used *do* matter. Note that the petition does not specify a particular medicine. The Creator knows exactly what you need, the dosage and the duration.

The Creator will not give you an energy correction that will harm you. You must, however, act responsibly because sometimes you may receive only a single energetic dose; the

Creator expects you to resume your normal medicine schedule. Ask the Creator if you can use this Petition.

The Miracle of Change

"People do not change, until the pain of not changing exceeds the pain of changing."

This describes our resistance to change. We resist anything we do not understand or that puts us at a disadvantage. When the emotional or physical pain is great enough, we usually take action to change our situation.

Let's look at the change that occurs during a healing. The mechanism for healing with Divine Love has been described previously. But something else happens:

As your body heals, your system begins a transformation to good health. A person in good health has a frequency between 439 Hz and 454 Hz.

As someone clears their spiritual limitations, their frequency increases in multiples of 454 Hz until they reach a threshold of 1816 Hz. This is indicative of a spiritual person who is capable of helping others to heal rapidly.

Wine and Water

In 1981 Marcel Vogel started a major research program that I participated in. In our private laboratory, one piece of equipment had a coil containing a proprietary crystalline device. The device was charged with a thought to improve the flavor of wine.

When we poured wine into the top of the coil, the crystalline device, through resonance transfer, charged the wine with a program that altered the chemistry of the wine, making it more flavorful.

Although water is something we often take for granted, it is not simply a combination of two hydrogen atoms and one oxygen atom, forming a compound that can exist as a solid, liquid, or gas.

Since the human body contains a great deal of water, it follows that the body can also be programmed. For many years, we demonstrated this doing spiritual energy healing using a crystalline device, freeing people from a variety of diseases which had no conventional medical solutions.

Through World Service Institute I have taught the general public how to do spiritual energy healing using only our petition system and Divine Love. As mentioned earlier, the findings were eventually combined into the AT ONENESS HEALING SYSTEM ADVANCED PROTOCOL.

Sending Divine Love to Others

When you are out in public and near people who need charging and balancing, their energy will draw upon yours, and it will feel as if your energy is being depleted. Instead of leaving the area and the people who are depleting your energy, hold the mental thought of charging and balancing the people around you. You will notice that both their energy levels and yours will be restored. Say quietly to yourself:

"With my spirit I accept Divine Love continuously throughout my entire being. I ask that the Creator send Divine Love continuously throughout my entire being and send the people Divine Love to help them according to the Creator's will."

Then lightly pulse your breath to put the Petition into place.

Energy In Water

There are exciting new frontiers for the application of energy in water.

An Australian experimenter discovered that with a particular equipment configuration he could capture energy from a battery, direct it into water, and use it to run gasoline engines without using gasoline fuel.

When this research was first revealed, great efforts were made to suppress the information. Nevertheless, home experimenters continue to make improvements, and now, many companies are investigating this "new" energy. In fact, it is *not* new energy, but a subset of the divine energy of the universe.

My book ACTIVATING DIVINE LOVE ENERGY IN WATER describes experiments structuring water, so that the water energy can be used to correct energetic imbalances in raw water.

These development programs are mentioned here so that interested readers can continue this research work, applying it for the betterment of mankind.

It is my belief that the energy of Divine Love represents all that is. What we consider to be different frequencies for communication and electronic equipment are subsets of Divine Love. And anything that tends to upset the balance of nature or harm mankind can be corrected by the proper application of Divine Love, with or without water as the transfer mechanism.

Healing With Divine Love In a Group

I have led groups to correct some environmental disasters and to redirect weather disasters.

146

We've corrected accidental poisoning from viruses that appear in water, completely dissolved oil slicks, and deactivated the harmful effect of a cyclone.

A Water Virus

A duck pond in San Jose, California had somehow picked up a virus that was killing the ducks. We sent Divine Love to the pond with the intention of preserving the ducks and making them well.

A day or two later it was reported that the virus was no longer in the pond. The water in the pond was intact, the virus was disassociated, and the ducks were well. The petition that we used was based on spiritual Divine Love applied to the physical kingdom.

Elimination of An Oil Slick

During a weekend workshop, one of the participants reported that an oil tanker had blown bilge oil off the coast of Rhode Island. The oil slick had come ashore and had coated the shoreline and all the wildlife.

With a group of 40 people, we focused on sending Divine Love to the water to dissolve the oil and to protect and clear all the wildlife.

Since we were some distance from the coast, we did not learn of the immediate effect until a day later. It was reported that, by some mysterious means, the oil slick had completely gone away in the afternoon. The water was clear and free of any oil slick, the beaches were clear and water fowl had no oil coating. Clearly the petition had been answered!

Disarming A Cyclone

At one time, I conducted internet healing programs (webinars) attended by people from all over the world. During one program, a woman from New Zealand revealed that she was anxious about a potential environmental disaster.

Apparently a cyclone was approaching the city of Wellington. She was concerned that the cyclone would create major damage in the downtown area, for example, by blowing out office building windows.

Fifty webinar attendees were logged in to the webinar from their respective home countries. I led the group in applying a petition to protect Wellington and it residents from the cyclone.

Very soon, our Wellington participant was able to describe IN REAL TIME how the winds suddenly calmed down, blowing gently through the city and causing no damage. Again, this is the power of Divine Love.

The Food Conundrum

It is well known that food crops are affected by pesticides, by bacteria, and by contaminated air and water. Yet even organically grown food, supposedly certified to be pesticide free, may be unsafe.

Before we identify what to do energetically, let's discuss energy in general. Everything is composed of energy. Consider the carrot: There is energy in the earth surrounding the carrot. There is energy associated with the carrot's healthy content. And there is the energy associated with any toxins affecting the carrot.

Washing fruits and vegetables does not eliminate toxins contained *inside* the carrot. However, because Divine Love is harmless to humans, it can operate at multiple spiritual frequencies to correct harmful things, including toxins, radiation, and human disease.

I believe that many of society's problems today contribute to poor health. So many people remain unaware of the health risks from foods, medicines, and unhealthy environments.

A divine solution is needed: One solution is to apply a healing technique to the food you consume, to the air you breathe, and to the places that you live in, work in, or visit.

At one time I believed that once something was subjected to a healing petition, its physical characteristics would be modified. With laboratory testing, I was surprised to learn that sometimes physical measurements: pH, temperature, mass spectrophotometry, compound identification, etc. would change, and sometimes they would not change at all.

In reviewing my notes I discovered that I had been using a petition to make a change, *but I had not included the Creator* in the petition. In some cases the frequency of Divine Love my body could process was not high enough to effect change.

When I used a petition that included the Creator and asked the Creator to do the healing, I got positive results. The general form of that Petition:

"With my spirit I send Divine Love into (the object) and ask the Creator to (state what you want to have happen) according to the Creator's will."

This clearly showed that there are two different kingdoms acting simultaneously. Remember that the spiritual kingdom always governs our physical kingdom.

Applying this information to food, I always say this before eating:

FOOD PETITION

This Petition may be said quietly, rather than aloud.

"With my spirit I send Divine Love into this food and ask the Creator to make this food safe for me to eat according to the Creator's will."

Remember to pulse breath lightly. And of course you can modify the above petition to include your entire family.

About Healing Rates

A common misconception about healing with Divine Love is that the process takes place instantly. Although there have been many examples of instantaneous healing, when you're working by yourself, your body is kept in energetic balance and heals at a rate that your spirit deems safe for you. Understanding how complex healing takes place is important.

Ordinarily, we apply Advanced Protocol Healing Statements to correct an issue. Although many people use Healing Statements to get quick results, during which they just sit back and let it happen, this does not take into consideration just how the body heals.

If nothing is interfering with you, healing can proceed at a normal rate, which may last hours, days, or weeks, depending upon the severity of the issue.

However, in the case of an injury, subtle background events, either before, during or after the injury, can prolong healing time and significantly reduce healing effectiveness.

➤   *At the time of an injury, we may react in anger or fear. That reaction produces an energetic block that can continue to build as we continue to generate negative thoughts. Negative thoughts are explained under "Correcting Unlovingness" in Chapter 4.*

Usually the Healing Statements will eliminate any injury energy blockages that occur, provided that you are using the Healing Statements soon after the injury. If you waited a week, and then started a Healing Statement to heal your injury, healing may be slower because of an increased build up of the energetic block.

The block will generally go to an area of your body that has been most recently weakened or injured. Then, while the Advanced Protocol is busy removing said energy block, you may be reinforcing the block with negative thoughts.

➤   *You may patiently wait for a healing to finish, but it does not happen because of the continuing energy block!*

The best way to address the problem is to assume that you have an energy blockage caused by your negative, unloving thinking. That blockage is frustrating healing. Use the appropriate Petitions to clear the problem.

Example of Delayed Healing

Let's say you have started an Advanced Protocol to correct a *sore knee*. There is a petition in the Protocol that removes *unlovingness* associated with the sore knee; you need not worry about what that unlovingness is.

Later on, you hurt your hand while taking out the garbage, but do not take action to heal the hand.

Over the next several days you become angry about something and that anger produces an unlovingness energy block. That energy block moves to the most recent weak point in your energy system, the injured hand. After a week of increasing hand pain, you decide to take action. You have two options:

1. Change the Advanced Protocol for your *sore knee*, replacing it using *hand pain* as the new

symptom in both Healing Statements. Then let the Advanced Protocol run to completion.

2. Alternatively, you might decide not to change the Advanced Protocol for your *sore knee,* instead saying a simple custom petition such as:

"W*ith my Spirit, I accept Divine Love continuously throughout my entire being. I ask that the Creator send Divine Love continuously throughout my entire being and reveal to me what is blocking my hand healing, remove the block, and heal my hand according to the Creator's will."*

If it is necessary for you to understand what the unlovingness block is, it will register in your consciousness. Wait a few hours.

If you do not get relief, ask the Creator what should be done for your hand to heal completely. The Creator may lead you to a different solution, such as releasing any unloving behavior feeding the energy block.

Once the energy blocks are out of your system, your hand will usually heal.

Effect of Pain Pills on Healing Rates

Pain pills are intended to deaden your pain sensors so that you no longer feel pain. Unfortunately, you also risk further injury to your body.

Divine Love is a spiritual healing process that functions differently from any pain medication. Divine Love removes both the pain and its underlying cause. You will immediately recognize that your petition is working.

Healing takes time whether or not you use a Divine Love technique. Remember, you do not control healing rates; your spirit and the Creator does.

If you have ever broken a bone, you know it takes 6 to 8 weeks or longer for it to heal. Adding a petition to act on your body generally speeds up the healing cycle. However, if you bombard your body with negative thoughts, fears, or doubts, that will slow your healing.

Try to be loving to yourself, not stressing over events in your life or in the world. How do you do this?

➤   *Use Healing Statements to remove all the causes of unlovingness from your system.*

This includes hate, fear, anger, envy, and any other negative feelings you may have. Take this approach to release unlovingness at least once a week until you recognize positive changes in your behavior.

Tissue Injuries

If you accidentally smash your finger while using a hammer, the result is generally a soft tissue injury that may take significant time to heal. Not only is there the potential for storing an emotional energy block, but it is unknown just how your immune system will respond.

Swelling controlled by the immune system and the brain, can be triggered inflammation. The swelling is basically water which is sent to the injured area for the purpose of protecting the damaged area while the body heals.

If you were to twist your wrist or ankle, you would probably see swelling that might take a long time to go down. If your emotions are also affecting the healing site, your recovery will be slower.

Remember that although swelling is a normal event, prolonged swelling limits healing. Use Divine Love petitions or the Advanced Protocol to remove the energy blocks. Then use the Advanced Protocol again to ask specifically for healing of the injury.

I have seen rapid healing of long-standing injuries that had not responded to medical treatment. This was usually because the *cause* included not only the original damage, but also the accumulated energy blocks.

➢ *When people ask the Creator for help AND address the underlying causes first, then ask for healing of the injury, rapid healing follows in most cases.*

I can attest to the significance of this because of my own injuries that required physical therapy. Doctors have been amazed by how rapidly my body recovered, only because I recognized the need to petition to remove underlying causes.

In some situations, clients may do everything right, but still experience slow healing. This may occur when the Creator wants you to give the body more time to heal, or the Creator delays the healing until we grasp a lesson being given.

Complex Illnesses

Many of today's health problems are killing people. It does not matter whether the illness comes from viruses, DNA modifications, the environment, or toxic poisoning.

Despite the many advances in science, we see increased rates of heart disease, diabetes, obesity, and other diseases which overload the immune system.

What is the solution?

The only solution that supersedes all other treatment possibilities is healing with Divine Love. If the Creator chooses to do so, your particular problem can be healed, provided that you reverently ask the Creator for help.

Medical science cannot correct or provide safe mechanisms to correct some of these illnesses.

➢ *Although it is not my intent to find fault with traditional medicine, in the absence of medical solutions, Divine Love may be the only solution. Thus, it is very important for everyone to establish a proper relationship with the Creator of the universe.*

Especially in the last 40 or 50 years, there have been many advances in technology. Computers and smart phones are everywhere, as are the communication techniques to operate them.

And yet we have abused technology in many ways.

Sadly, the detrimental effects of electronic devices are generally not well studied and not well regulated. Thus, people may contract environmental illnesses from their continual exposure to electromagnetic radiation, and that radiation can create poisonous toxins in the body.

Hopefully we will eventually better understand these detrimental effects and be able to make changes before such illnesses increase.

It is one thing to *inadvertently* be exposed to something that is not good for us, but it is far better to be aware of the dangers in order to actively avoid them.

Many adults, regardless of their sophistication and education, are like small children, interested only in what is right in front of us, oblivious to the dangers of our world.

Let's Review Some Key Points

Those of you who have embraced healing with Divine Love know that you can release not only negative emotions, but also the underlying causes of most emotions and illnesses.

You can resolve most problems by applying the techniques given in our video, ADVANCED PROTOCOL AND HEALING STATEMENT TRAINING VIDEO, or in the book DYNAMIC REALITIES AND DIVINE LOVE HEALING.

These resources, in addition to other videos and materials on our website, will generally provide what you need to change your life and your environment.

Since these are not normal times, be aware that you may inadvertently STOP healing due to some accumulated fear-driven stress.

We are not able to function lovingly when we experience *excessive negative emotions.* Then our Spirit may stop our healing until we recognize that our negative behavior is frustrating our wellness.

Correcting Problems

When you have used Advanced Protocol Healing Statements ONCE for a given symptom, together with the associated breathing exercises, notice how you feel.

➢ If there is no improvement in a few hours, restart your healing by using the following Petition every time you feel a negative emotion:

"With my Spirit, I accept Divine Love continuously throughout my entire being. I ask the Creator to send Divine Love continuously throughout my entire being. I ask the Creator to heal whatever is preventing my wellness according to the Creator's will."

Use the above Petition as many times daily as you need to attain comfort. This Petition removes your internal stress without the need to identify each issue.

Are you achieving beneficial results using the Advanced Protocol? If not, you may not be aware of THREE QUESTIONS that must be understood to achieve a Divine Love spiritual healing:

1. What really happens when you specify an AT ONENESS HEALING SYSTEM ADVANCED PROTOCOL symptom?

As explained earlier, when the symptom you select corresponds with what the Creator wants to have happen in your system, your symptom starts healing. The healing applies to your spirit, soul, other energy fields, and your physical cells.

However, when you use a symptom that does not fit with what is needed in your body at a particular time, the healing of your specified symptom may be suspended. Instead, Divine Love works in conjunction with your spirit to address any adverse energy in your system that is, or can become, *life threatening*. You may not think that anything is happening because something that might harm you may not yet have manifested with recognizable symptoms.

The good news: Once any harmful energy is neutralized, the Advanced Protocol continues to address your originally specified symptom.

2. When a symptom in the Advanced Protocol does not result in healing within a reasonable amount of time, what does it mean?

It usually means the Creator of the universe wants you to recognize and act upon the root cause of your illness. In almost every case where healing is withheld, it is because a person does not recognize how their *continued unloving behavior* adversely affects their health.

If you have not developed a close working relationship with the Creator, or are afraid of making that contact, or believe such contact is impossible, you may be stuck in your limited belief system. This leaves you unable to identify what is causing your problem.

As explained in Chapter 4, to become unstuck, simply ask the Creator directly for help to understand what the issue is, and what you must change in yourself to permanently correct the problem.

Remember to give yourself permission, both to let go of the root cause of the symptom and to accept the healing. Healing then becomes a cooperative effort between you and the Creator.

3. Do you have doubts regarding the existence of a Divine Creator?

Belief in the Creator is strengthened for most people when they see health improvements.

Conversely, when people refuse to acknowledge the existence of the Creator of the universe, it has been my experience that they cannot successfully experience a healing with Divine Love.

4. Do people who continually and knowingly do unloving things in their lives have poor results?

Energetic blockages increase and strengthen with continued unloving behavior.

Most harmful behaviors against people or nature are forgiven by the Creator, provided that one ASKS sincerely for forgiveness from the Creator.

At Oneness Healing System
Advanced Protocol Status

The AT ONENESS HEALING SYSTEM ADVANCED PROTOCOL is a powerful spiritual healing tool that has evolved over 30 years of intense spiritual development. We believe the Advanced Protocol is an effective healing system, helping people in many countries recover from illness.

"If you don't like the road you're walking, start paving another one."

- Dolly Parton

CHAPTER 7

THE LARGEST MIRACLE

Many people don't realize the implications of the many side effects from the COVID virus that have been introduced to humanity. Research scientists and others throughout the world have developed treatments for COVID. Some treatments have been successful, but not others.

Now we are seeing a number of side effects from those treatments, side effects resulting in serious illness and even death. For example, insurance companies in the United States are reporting a dramatic increase in unexpected early death rates among teenagers.

Side effects are also harming adults, and many of these side effects do not respond to normal medical treatments, even with today's advanced technology.

Regrettably, the reporting of these harmful side effects is woefully understated. It seems that once people have weakened immune systems, they no longer respond well to conventional treatments. If this trend continues unchecked over the next several years, we would expect to see a significant increase in deaths from those side effects.

I believe the only solution lies in an appeal to the Creator for help. Just how we do that is the subject of this chapter.

The techniques that we teach have evolved since 1980. The information has been given to help build a foundation for understanding the many elements of Divine Love.

People advance at a pace that is suited to them. When new technologies and healing techniques are introduced, it takes time to learn their uses.

People more readily accept new concepts and new technology products once they understand how to utilize them,

Divine Love spiritual healing is an example of a new concept. We have advanced this state-of-the-art energy healing through careful study and trial and error, resulting in the AT ONENESS HEALING SYSTEM ADVANCED PROTOCOL. The Protocol can be used to correct almost anything, but to be successful one must follow the guidelines.

My role as a teacher is to present the facts, allowing you to determine how the Advanced Protocol responds to your needs. Many people, including medical researchers, doctors from many disciplines, and the general public have contacted me over the years for additional understanding. Imagine someone who has a debilitating disease learning about a spiritual solution involving the Creator of the universe, a solution that transcends anything else that mankind can offer.

You will most likely have formed a positive opinion of the Advanced Protocol if you have used it successfully. I know this is true because our teaching methods are spreading throughout the world and are being used in more than 35 countries.

Our clients know that even though the Advanced Protocol is available to people via our videos and books, billions of people throughout the world know nothing about Divine Love and have little knowledge regarding the Creator of the universe.

I have asked the Creator repeatedly over the years what message I can bring forward to help people, because I realize that often when people are afraid and are ill, they do not know how to ask the Creator for help.

The Creator told me that the Advanced Protocol is to be brought forward as a teaching tool to help people, not only to recover health, but also to respect the spiritual realm and to generate love for all people. I am honored to be part of that effort.

Three conditions are discussed in this chapter:

1. Applying Custom Healing techniques to deal with current problems.

2. The role of the Advanced Protocol.

3. Helping others ask the Creator for help.

Custom Healing Techniques

We believe energy healers might increase their effectiveness simply by incorporating Divine Love Custom Petitions into their practices.

Shamans, Indian medicine men, Tibetan monks and other energy healers definitely produce healing effects. However, many techniques were developed to heal people individually or in small groups. For that reason, and because of secrecy associated with some of those healing techniques, the general public does not have a basis for understanding spiritual healing.

I have tried a variety of healing systems. For many years I taught group healing techniques, where the group could heal one or more clients. We learned that a fairly large number of people are needed in group healing to produce positive effects across a large geographic area.

> *And those techniques are not effective against major health events affecting billions of people globally. Now we are trying to help restore people to the health conditions they had prior to the arrival of the COVID virus.*

> *However, we lack a way to share this spiritual healing information worldwide.*

Role of the Advanced Protocol

The Advanced Protocol requires the client to specify a *symptom* which is then used in the Protocol. Prior to the COVID virus, we defined a symptom as something a client emotionally or physically experienced, such as a body pain. One difficulty is that people are developing one or more life-threatening symptoms, some of which may manifest instantaneously, while others may appear later. Yet when the immune system is failing unexpectedly, we cannot assume that we are able to specify the *correct* symptoms to use.

We need a more *general symptom* so that the Creator can direct healing without interference. Only the Creator truly knows us and can provide exactly what we need.

I asked the Creator how to word the symptom and was told to use: "*covid-related symptoms.*"
Once the two Healing Statements are activated, clients need to do deep breathing to assure that their bodies oxygenate properly, as explained previously.

We know that when people discover something that works correctly, that information spreads rapidly. In this way, we can utilize the Advanced Protocol as a healing and teaching tool to help people understand the importance of the spiritual realm and Divine Love.

In this case there is no provision for a Custom Petition because the Advanced Protocol has petitions that maintain a safe balance in the body.

How can we get the word out to the billions of people who have never heard of the Advanced Protocol, Divine Love, or healing with Divine Love? One solution is presented below.

How We Can Help Others

I asked the Creator how masses of people could be helped and was told that all they have to do is earnestly ask the Creator for help. Once it is accepted that a spiritual realm feeds information into, then changes the physical realm, one realizes that all things are possible to those who believe in the Creator.

People can act as proxies for all humanity by acknowledging the Creator, and by asking the Creator for help. Over time, this should help create a better standard for living based upon loving our fellow man and understanding how to work with the Creator.

Following is the simple petition I propose. Say this aloud whenever and wherever you like. Pulse your breath to release it into what is called the "mass consciousness," which serves all humanity.

PROXY PETITION

Say aloud:

"With my spirit I accept Divine Love continuously throughout my entire being. I ask the Creator to send Divine Love continuously throughout my entire being and help the people of the world to connect with the Creator and receive the Creator's healing according to the Creator's will."

Remember to pulse breath.

"Your best is going to change
from moment to moment;
it will be different when you
are healthy as opposed to sick.
Under any circumstances,
simply do your best,
and you will avoid
self-judgment,
self-abuse and regret."

- Don Miguel Ruiz

CHAPTER 8

PROBLEM SOLVING
WITH THE
MIRACLE OF DIVINE LOVE

This entire book has been predicated on showing you how to build a relationship with the Creator, working with Divine Love and the Creator to facilitate change. This process is not limited to health problems.

Huge social problems exist in most countries of the world and most of us would like to see solutions to these problems.

In this chapter we identify some unresolved social problems and describe a few ways to make effective changes possible.

Spiritual Warfare

Some non-spiritual forces in the world are a mix of evil-minded individuals and poorly evolved souls. These forces seek to overcome the spiritual forces of Divine Love and the Creator. Although they won't be successful, these non-spiritual forces currently make life discouraging for many people.

Do you ever wonder about these social problems:

Gun violence in schools.
The increased use of addictive drugs.
Rage-fueled violence.
"New" diseases with no medical cures.

These are but a few of the issues confronting us today. Spiritual warfare is being conducted on several levels of consciousness. Those attempting to manipulate you may also attempt to discredit you and your opinions. We see this when social media content is posted but suddenly removed. "Bad actors" responsible for the above problems bombard us with their destructive thoughts and actions.

Since the COVID pandemic lockdowns began, the isolation from family and friends has created much unhappiness. There is discord between governments and their citizenry, between many companies and their employees, and, especially disturbing, between family members.

Human beings need loving contact with each other and much of that has been denied under lockdown rules.

To eliminate much of the divisiveness that is occurring, we each need to accept and experience Divine Love in our daily lives and to use Divine Love Petitions for any problematic situations. It is essential that we include, and be guided by, the Creator in all that we think and do.

We will explain how to integrate information in this chapter so that people who choose to work together in groups can be more effective. But should you choose to work by yourself the approach is the same.

Clear Communications Are Essential

Everyone wants to communicate clearly with others. And, although most people believe they are clear communicators, we are often unaware of our many personality factors that interfere with clear communication. This adversely affects our ability to properly relate to others and to achieve our objectives.

Group Participation

While many of our readers are active members of organizations in their communities, others have no experience in dealing with large social problems, and some people just find comfort in working by themselves.

Once we understand various courses of action to effect social change, we can begin to help make changes, whether we operate in groups or by ourselves.

I have learned that when the Creator is involved in either personal or group decision making, both understanding and the ability to function increase, producing outstanding results.

To address a social problem, we can ask the Creator for guidance utilizing a simple petition. However, some social problems require a larger group effort to effectively implement solutions.

Of course the key is to actively involve the Creator in your efforts; the answers coming forth will be divinely guided by the Creator. We must apply our best efforts to integrate that guidance.

Research on behavioral science and management techniques reveals that:

➢ *A group working together can come to better problem solutions more quickly, and with higher success rates, than individuals working alone.*

Many people have not learned how to identify, analyze, and apply the skills needed to solve problems, so let's discuss behavioral traits that will help us engage with others. Our objective is to provide the tools for you to successfully participate in group problem solving.

Following are two key sections to help you better understand and apply Divine Love in your daily dealings, whether operating by yourself or with a group.

Requirements For Success

Common Passion. A group should be enthusiastic and truly passionate about the objective.

Focus. A clear statement of intent should be in place before a group is formed. When a group comes together for the first time, they may have only a vague idea of the goals, or wrongly expect to advance their own projects and beliefs.

Commitment. Gather people with experience in the appropriate field. Some desired attributes:

Sufficient education to meet the challenges; outspoken, able to express an opinion; unimpressed by status; respectful of others; and known as achievers, not theoreticians.

Unity. The group should operate as a unit. Any success is a group success based on group effort.

Group Leaders. Every group needs a physical spokesperson capable of dealing with people inside and outside of the group. That person is called a *physical* Group Leader. The Leader may be either appointed or elected. A Group Leader must also have the skills needed to evaluate the Group and its efforts.

The *spiritual* Group Leader is the Creator. When the group works together, solutions are provided by whatever means the Creator employs. Such guidance is given to the entire group, not just the physical Group Leader.

Build the Right Group Dynamics

A group dynamic includes a published set of agreed-upon operating conditions, designed to put everyone at ease. The components of the dynamics include:

Equal votes. Group members should be able to share their opinions freely, without ridicule or recrimination and know that their opinions are valued. The titles and positions of members should not be a consideration.

No hidden agendas. From the beginning, group members must trust that they are working on the real problem and that they are not being used as political pawns for any hidden agenda.

No secrets. Group members need not share personal information, although understanding the problems of others, e.g., a death in the family, can improve the group's interpersonal communications. Of course, any secrets that might influence decisions should not be withheld from the group.

Openness and candor. It is important that Group members express themselves and not try to please anyone else. Sometimes a group member does not openly communicate for fear of hurting feelings. This behavior trait corrects as the group utilizes the petition with guidance from the Creator.

Group Leader's expectations. Do not begin until the Group Leader is able to share a clear vision of the mission and the problems to be solved. The Group Leader should be confident that each group member understands the charge and any constraints.

Leadership style. The Group Leader must act as a facilitator, not a dictator exerting control over the group. Group Leaders should not seek personal recognition; accolades for success belong to the group as a whole.

Final decisions. After agreement in principle among all group members, if some issues remain unresolved, the Group Leader, with the Creator's approval, is responsible for the final decision. All decisions must be made in a professional manner.

Other dynamics. To solve huge social problems we absolutely need the Creator's guidance; other group dynamics will also be managed under the Creator's guidance.

Decision making. Making decisions that have been influenced by friends, family members, colleagues, politicians,, journalists, or others, can lead to chaos. External forces may affect that chaos, but it is more often the result of unlovingness and the exclusion of the Creator from the decision making process.

When we involve the Creator directly in our decision-making, we receive solutions that are supported by the Creator. For example:

➢   All results are driven by the mutual spiritual efforts of the group and solutions seem to develop effortlessly.

➢   Obstacles to progress disappear and there is no resistance to change.

➢   Solutions are organized with ease.

➢   Group dynamics and personalities align.

➤ When "right" spiritual decisions are made, the correct outcome is produced in spite of chaos.

Achieving Spiritual Guidance When Building Groups

Our individual egos and opinions sometimes interfere with our ability to see the larger picture. The above guidelines for group activities remind us to be tolerant of other viewpoints and help us understand what other group members are trying to communicate.

To overcome any limitations, begin each meeting with everyone reciting the following petition out loud. Wait for several minutes while the petition aligns the group with the Creator. This process ensures that:

➤ *Everything is done in a loving way for the betterment of the group.*

➤ *Any solution that is proposed by the group is with the Creator's direct spiritual participation and guidance.*

➢ *Differences in personalities and behaviors will have no affect on communication or on group dynamics.*

These principles can also be applied in families, in your workplace, in social groups, or in any other group.

Building Groups Petition

Say out loud, and all together:

"With my spirit I accept Divine Love continuously throughout my entire being and ask the Creator to send Divine Love continuously throughout my entire being. Our group acknowledges the individuality of the members and ask that the Creator resolve any issues in the Group and guide us to make good decisions according to the Creator's will." Then everyone should pulse breath to activate and release the Petition.

In Closing

I sincerely hope that you will choose to apply these principles in your own life to help yourself, your family, your business, your government, and the world.

"Love one another and help others
rise to the higher levels,
simply by pouring out love.
Love is infectious and
the greatest healing energy."

- Sai Baba

PUTTING IT ALL TOGETHER

This has been an in-depth presentation of Divine Love spiritual healing and its components.

The Advanced Protocol should help you attain favorable healing results. As we have mentioned throughout this book, your healing success depends upon your relationship with the Creator of the universe. You are solely responsible for your own behavior and any changes to that behavior; those positive changes lead to healing.

We have explained how all of these petitions work to help you. And, we have emphasized the importance of deep breathing so that healing proceeds more rapidly.

Petitions in this book have been modified to help you align with the Creator for more rapid healing. That alignment lessens the impact of emotional and other energy blocks.

You have learned how to use symptoms in both Custom Petitions and the Advanced Protocol.

Over the years, various healing methods have been presented as *mental* or *personal* love methods for healing. Yet my Divine Love spiritual healing work over more than 40 years has proven to me that the Creator's Divine Love surrounds us and is readily available. The Creator's Divine Love is the source of true healing.

Millions of people worldwide are in need of healing, but do not have the guidance needed to be successful. Many do not have a spiritual connection to the Creator, and many simply do not know how to ask the Creator for help.

We can all be of service to our spiritual brothers and sisters by petitioning the Creator to help those who do not have access to Divine Love methods. You may use the petition found at the end of Chapter 7 to establish a worldwide petition.

"It is in your hands
to make a better world
for all who live in it."

- Nelson Mandela

"Don't settle for average.
Bring your best to the moment.
Then, whether it fails or
succeeds, at least you know
you gave it all you had."

- Angela Bassett

ADDENDUM

REMOVING DIMENSIONAL VIBRATIONS

Synopsis

Because the Advanced Protocol takes care of Dimensional Vibrations, we do not deal with them as before. However, since some people like to understand the origins of their illnesses, this chapter offers a more comprehensive look at this phenomenon.

The concept of Dimensional Vibrations is based upon energetic principles from the past and the present that affect current health. Dimensional Vibrations are underlying energy blocks that cause cells to suddenly stop working properly, or cause swelling in the body, or prevent healing. Until Dimensional Vibrations are released healing does not occur.

Many years ago I learned about Dimensional Vibrations from my Angels and was told that the human spirit transcends multiple lives.

➤ *As each successive generation lives, their energetic forms experience transitions commonly considered DNA modifications.*

As we think about DNA, we should realize that over time, our DNA has indeed been affected by our forefathers.

Scientists have determined that damaged DNA can be repaired by gene sequencing. However, any DNA changes initiated by gene sequencing may introduce potentially irreversible side effects. Thorough testing over many years is needed to evaluate the long-term effects.

➤ *The Creator can rapidly change one condition to another, as I've seen with some difficult Divine Love cases.*

Three different DNA conditions may adversely affect us:

1. DNA damage we have inherited from our ancestors.

2. DNA damage we have incurred because of our choices in this lifetime.

3. DNA damage and limited healing we have incurred from past life episodes.

What To Do

When I asked the Creator to explain to me what the Creator's will was for those three conditions, I received this information:

➢ *DNA damage inherited from ancestors is correctable if that is the Creator's will.*

➢ *DNA damage incurred because of poor choices in this lifetime is correctable if that is the Creator's will AND if the individual accepts responsibility to change behavior.*

➢ All who believe in the Creator will be helped, depending upon the Creator's will, AND provided that they ask the Creator for help.

➢ Some illnesses are correctable when the root cause of those illnesses is unloving behavior in this lifetime. (This was true in about half of the cancer cases we have worked on.)

➢ When someone has developed multiple illnesses because of toxicity in their DNA, those illnesses may be approved for a correction according to the Creator's will.

➢ In all cases, the petitioner must ask the Creator to be forgiven, or there may be no healing.

➢ Damaged DNA is usually not correctable from the physical realm because the underlying cause is spiritual rather than physical. Divine Love corrects spiritual damage in the spiritual realm and that correction is passed down into the physical realm, resulting in healing.

Correcting the Past

Some considerations:

When someone asks the Creator to forgive their unloving behavior and to heal symptoms, the unlovingness is generally forgiven and health improves.

If we neglect properly caring for our planet and our bodies, some reeducation may be required. We need to ask the Creator for guidance and we need to follow that guidance.

If you have done everything on the physical level as instructed, but you are still suffering, then you must again ask the Creator for help.

We have reached a point in the development of humanity where people throughout the world must make a choice:

➢ *Align spiritually with the Creator and work with the Creator to improve health and our physical world, or,*

➢   *Continue to make unloving, self-serving choices that harm others, then deal with the consequences.*

In 2021 I asked the Creator whether people whose DNA was being damaged by the COVID virus and subsequent treatment side effects could be helped.

I was told that if people asked the Creator for help, their DNA and health would be restored to the conditions of their bodies before the virus experience.

People would also need to ask the Creator for guidance and healing for any other preexisting conditions.

If we can lessen healing time by asking the Creator right now for help, why worry about clearing out our Dimensional Vibrations? The answer is in what happens to us during a typical healing with Divine Love:

➢   *If the Creator wants to preserve your health, it is done with minimum effort on your part other than correcting your unloving behavior.*

➤ *If the Creator wants you to be aware of any DNA modifications that may have been passed down to you, then addressing the Dimensional Vibrations becomes essential. Those Dimensional Vibrations can interfere with your health recovery until you acknowledge them and willingly release them to the Creator.*

➤ *Fortunately, when using the Advanced Protocol, Dimensional Vibrations are removed automatically.*

Some people use the Dimensional Vibration method to discover the underlying cause for a symptom. With the assistance of a guardian Angel they return to a time when the underlying cause was identified.

➤ *If you believe that Divine Love applies exactly the right frequency and power to beneficially change your DNA, isn't that* motivation for you to engage with the Creator to restore your health?

Removing Dimensional Vibrations

Sit comfortably by yourself where there are no distractions, including cellphones. Put your feet flat on the floor. Do not cross your arms and legs at any time during this process.

If you are uncomfortable with the process, ask the Creator to assign an Angel to accompany you and to explain the meaning of the dimensional vibration you see in your mind's eye.

Say aloud this Petition:

DIMENSIONAL VIBRATION
REMOVAL PETITION

"With my spirit, my assigned Angel and Divine Love, I go backwards in time. I ask the Creator to show me the Dimensional Vibration responsible for my limited healing or health problem."

This may take several minutes so be patient. Once you sense an event, or see an image in your mind's eye, ask your Angel to help you to understand how that affects your life and DNA today.

Then, ask the Creator for forgiveness for your involvement. Next, focus on the image with Divine Love and ask that the underlying condition be dissolved by the Creator.

If the Creator grants your petition, the dimensional vibration will dissolve.

Ask your Angel to identify if another dimensional vibration is limiting your healing. If so, go further back in time until you reach that image and repeat the request for forgiveness and dissolution of that dimensional vibration.

It is possible you could have two, three, or more dimensional vibrations affecting a single health condition. You have finished when your Angel tells you there is nothing more.

Next, consciously draw in your breath and bring yourself back to the present day. Relax for a few minutes reflecting on what you've just learned before proceeding to the next step.

If you have not yet asked the Creator for help, review Chapter Four and the section "Asking the Creator for Help."

Statement of Use

Custom Petitions: Do use the DIMENSIONAL VIBRATION REMOVAL PETITION as given. This procedure is generally used by people who are using Divine Love to correct long-standing symptoms, but who are not using the Advanced Protocol. Ask the Creator if you should use this procedure before you try it.

Advanced Protocol: Dimensional vibrations are pop ups handled by the Advanced Protocol, so there is no need to remove individual dimensional vibrations.

CHAKRA AND THYMUS
HEALING METHODS

In addition to the Advanced Protocol, two other Divine Love methods may be useful, especially for people using their own healing systems.

Ask the Creator if you should use either of these methods and follow the guidance.

Chakra Healing

The Advanced Protocol works to effect healing of a specified symptom. For example, suppose that while you are patiently waiting for the Advanced Protocol to complete the healing of a cancer that you have specified as a symptom, you develop an unrelated pain in your shoulder. What can you do?

You could change the Healing Statement symptom specified in the Advanced Protocol to deal with the shoulder pain. If you do that, the cancer healing stops, and the Advanced Protocol begins working on the shoulder pain. Then, when the shoulder pain is healed, the Advanced Protocol resumes correcting the cancer.

However, if you are working on something with the Advanced Protocol and do not want to modify that protocol symptom, you might use chakra healing to deal with the shoulder pain. A block in a chakra is the same as a *pop up* energy block in the Advanced Protocol.

Clearing and healing an energy-blocked chakra can produce an immediate reduction in pain if the shoulder pain originates in one of the 14 key chakras. In the meantime, the Advanced Protocol operates when a chakra is not being examined or healed.

In India and some other countries, chakra healing is fairly well understood. Unfortunately, for much of the world, it is not only misunderstood, but often taught improperly.

Chakra healing is not a substitute for using the Advanced Protocol or for asking the Creator for help. Also, please try it only with the Creator's guidance.

Our 14 main chakras are energy ports connecting with the internal energy system of the body. The seven key chakras on the front of the body control the front and seven identical chakras on the back of the body control the back of the body.

Always begin a chakra healing on the *front* and center line of the body. The first chakra is located behind the sex glands in the pelvic area. The second chakra is located about 2 inches below the navel. The third chakra is located at the solar plexus. The fourth chakra is located in line with the sternum at the level of your heart. The fifth chakra is located at the throat above the collarbone. The sixth chakra, also known as "the third eye," is located slightly above and between the eyebrows. The seventh chakra is located on the crown of the head.

The first chakra front and first chakra back share the same location.

The seventh chakra front and seventh chakra back share the same location.

The second through sixth chakras front are directly in line horizontally with the second through sixth chakras back.

➢   *Using a petition, chakra healing focuses intention into each chakra in turn to identify anything that is causing a symptom.*

Begin with the first chakra front. When that chakra is clear, move on to the second chakra front and so forth on the front side. When the seventh chakra front is clear, wait a few minutes before beginning the chakra clearing for the first chakra back through the seventh chakra back.

The general form of a chakra petition is:

"With my spirit and Divine Love I focus into the (chakra location) and ask the Creator to identify all underlying causes interfering with the healing of (state the related symptom) and to release and heal all those underlying causes and related symptoms according to the Creator's will."

In our example, a *sore shoulder* is the symptom. For the first chakra front the complete petition would be:

With my spirit and Divine Love I focus into the first chakra front and ask the Creator to identify all underlying causes interfering with the healing of my sore shoulder and to release and heal all those underlying causes and related symptoms according to the Creator's will."

If there is an energy block in that first chakra front, it will be felt as pressure or a vibration at that location.

➢   *To activate each chakra petition, pulse your breath once with your mouth closed. Do deep breathing for one minute; any sensation should then be gone.*

It is important to do the chakra clearing in the proper sequence. An underlying cause may be located in one or more of the 14 chakras. And, multiple underlying causes may be located in the same chakra for the symptom (shoulder pain).

Since you may not feel anything moving in your body, it would be wise to spend one full minute on each chakra doing deep breathing after you have pulsed your breath. If there is another underlying cause in the same chakra, it will become known to you and you can repeat the petition and the breath pulse.

Waiting one minute after you pulse your breath allows your body time to recover.

After one minute, breathe in and withdraw your attention from the chakra you were clearing. Take a few deep breaths to relax then breathe out and go into the next chakra, again using the general petition.

To eliminate errors, following are the exact petitions to use for each of the 14 chakras. When you identify and release the energy blocks in the chakras, you will experience a reduction in your symptom.

➢ *Do not stop chakra healing just because the symptom may have lessened; there may be* another underlying cause in that same chakra or in another chakra.

Here is the correct wording for the 14 chakras:

"With my spirit and Divine Love I focus into the first chakra front and ask the Creator to identify all underlying causes interfering with the healing of my sore shoulder and to release and heal all those underlying causes and related symptoms according to the Creator's will."

"With my spirit and Divine Love I focus into the second chakra front and ask the Creator to identify all underlying causes interfering with the healing of my sore shoulder and to release and heal all those underlying causes and related symptoms according to the Creator's will."

"With my spirit and Divine Love I focus into the third chakra front and ask the Creator to identify all underlying causes interfering with the healing of my sore shoulder and to release and heal all those underlying causes and related symptoms according to the Creator's will."

"With my spirit and Divine Love I focus into the fourth chakra front and ask the Creator to identify all underlying causes interfering with the healing of my sore shoulder and to release and heal all those underlying causes and related symptoms according to the Creator's will."

"With my spirit and Divine Love I focus into the fifth chakra front and ask the Creator to identify all underlying causes interfering with the healing of my sore shoulder and to release and heal all those underlying causes and related symptoms according to the Creator's will."

"With my spirit and Divine Love I focus into the sixth chakra front and ask the Creator to identify all underlying causes interfering with the healing of my sore shoulder and to release and heal all those underlying causes and related symptoms according to the Creator's will."

"With my spirit and Divine Love I focus into the seventh chakra front and ask the

Creator to identify all underlying causes interfering with the healing of my sore shoulder and to release and heal all those underlying causes and related symptoms according to the Creator's will."

"With my spirit and Divine Love I focus into the first chakra back and ask the Creator to identify all underlying causes interfering with the healing of my sore shoulder and to release and heal all those underlying causes and related symptoms according to the Creator's will."

"With my spirit and Divine Love I focus into the second chakra back and ask the Creator to identify all underlying causes interfering with the healing of my sore shoulder and to release and heal all those underlying causes and related symptoms according to the Creator's will."

"With my spirit and Divine Love I focus into the third chakra back and ask the Creator to identify all underlying causes interfering with the healing of my sore shoulder and to release *and heal all those underlying causes and related symptoms according to the Creator's will."*

"With my spirit and Divine Love I focus into the fourth chakra back and ask the Creator to identify all underlying causes interfering with the healing of my sore shoulder and to release and heal all those underlying causes and related symptoms according to the Creator's will."

"With my spirit and Divine Love I focus into the fifth chakra back and ask the Creator to identify all underlying causes interfering with the healing of my sore shoulder and to release and heal all those underlying causes and related symptoms according to the Creator's will."

"With my spirit and Divine Love I focus into the sixth chakra back and ask the Creator to identify all underlying causes interfering with the healing of my sore shoulder and to release and heal all those underlying causes and related symptoms according to the Creator's will."

"With my spirit and Divine Love I focus into the seventh chakra back and ask the Creator to

identify all underlying causes interfering with the healing of my sore shoulder and to release and heal all those underlying causes and related symptoms according to the Creator's will."

Remember to pulse your breath once each time you use one of the chakra petitions. Your pulsed breath releases the petition into your total energy field so that healing can occur.

Many health problems are correctable through these 14 key chakra points, but there are even more chakras throughout the body. A good yoga book will detail the location of those chakras.

Statement of Use

Custom Petitions: Ask the Creator if chakra healing methods should be used to release energy blocks.

Advanced Protocol: The Protocol usually automatically clears chakra energy blocks as pop ups. Ask the Creator if you should also use chakra healing methods to clear chakra energy blocks.

Thymus Healing

In 1980 we discovered that a symptom could be addressed through one location in particular: the thymus gland. The thymus, an important part of the immune system, connects energetically to everything in the body. The thymus is located in the front part of the chest directly behind the sternum and between the lungs, about 2 inches below the juncture of the collarbone and sternum.

When would thymus healing be used instead of chakra healing? With chakra healing, the exact locations for underlying causes are identified.

Thymus healing accesses only one position, which means that if there are multiple underlying causes, clearing takes longer. The general petition would look like this:

"With my spirit I accept Divine Love into my thymus and throughout my entire being. I ask that the Creator send Divine Love throughout my entire being. I ask the Creator to identify all underlying causes interfering with the healing

of my (state the symptom) and to release and heal all my underlying causes and my (symptom) according to the Creator's will."

Close your mouth, breathe in, pulse your breath outward once through your nose. Then do deep breathing for 30 minutes or longer until the condition has completely cleared.

If you had a *headache*, the complete petition would look like this:

"With my spirit I accept Divine Love into my thymus and throughout my entire being. I ask that the Creator send Divine Love throughout my entire being. I ask the Creator to identify all underlying causes interfering with the healing of my headache and to release and heal all underlying causes and my headache according to the Creator's will."

Close your mouth, breathe in, pulse your breath outward once through your nose.

Thymus healing has only been used and tested when doing crystal healing. It should not be used unless much additional healing time is available.

Statement of Use

Custom Petitions: Ask the Creator if the thymus healing method should be used.

Advanced Protocol: Do not use thymus healing because the Advanced Protocol already contains everything needed.

Special Thanks:

To the Creator and my Angels who provide me both guidance and understanding as we strive to help humanity become more loving.

To my manuscript reviewers Faith Supple, Robin Hucks and Faith Ann Fritchie: Thank you for your excellent contributions.

I hope all who read this book will share it with friends and loved ones. May the peace and Divine Love of the Creator be with you always!

Ingram Content Group UK Ltd.
Milton Keynes UK
UKHW011834200423
420514UK00001B/149